SOUP
Glorious soup

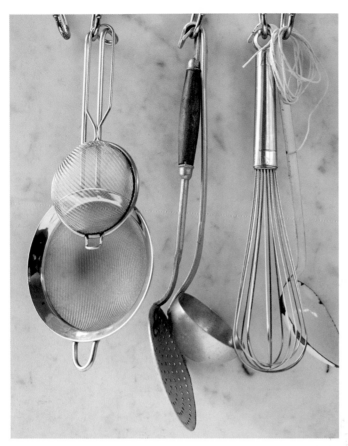

SOUP
Glorious soup

Annie Bell

Photography by Richard Jung

Kyle Cathie Limited

For Rothko

First published in Great Britain in 2010 by Kyle Cathie Limited, 23, Howland Street, London W1T 4AY

general.enquiries@kyle-cathie.com www.kylecathie.com ISBN: 978 1 85626 913 1

A CIP catalogue record for this title is available from the British Library

Annie Bell is hereby identified as the author of this work in accordance with Section 77 of the Copyright, Designs and Patents Act 1988

Editor: Vicky Orchard *Design:* Jane Humphrey *Photography:* Richard Jung *Styling:* Gabi Tubbs *Food styling:* Annie Rigg
Copy editor: Catherine Ward *Production:* Gemma John

Colour reproduction by Sang Choy in Singapore
Printed in China by C&C Offset Printing Co., Ltd.

ACKNOWLEDGMENTS Many thanks to those small independent shops who keep the flag flying, and who kindly allowed us to photograph within:
Patricia Michelson and La Fromagerie, Marylebone; Fiona O'Callaghan and James Knight of Mayfair; David House, Glen Kirton
and Allens butcher, and Charlie Boxer and Italo Deli.
With many thanks to Kyle Cathie and Judith Hannam, Commissioning Editor, to Vicky Orchard, Editor, to Julia Barder, Sales and Marketing Director, and
to Victoria Scales for publicity. With particular thanks also to Jane Humphrey for designing the book, to Gabi Tubbs for her
art direction, to Richard Jung for the photography, to Annie Rigg for cooking and presenting the dishes, and to Rachel Wood, also to Angela Mason.
And as ever, to Jonnie, Louis and Rothko, for settling to bowl after bowl over many years.

Contents

Introduction 6

The Greengrocer 8

The Dairy 44

The Fishmonger 70

The Butcher 100

The Grocer 126

The Baker 150

Stocks 168

Index 174

◈ A recent American university study came to the conclusion that we can all be defined as particular character types depending on our soup preference. Aside from marvelling that any educational establishment can find the resources to carry out this kind of research, it left me feeling I must be suffering from a personality disorder. I for one cannot choose. Asked to name a favourite between a smooth silky onion soup, gazpacho, a mealy lentil soup, a thin hot and sour Thai broth, a luxurious garlic-rich *bourride*, a chicken noodle soup and a smoked haddock chowder, I would be left tongue-tied and dithering. Thankfully I don't have to.

Soup encompasses every possible conception of liquid, and increasingly not-so-liquid sustenance, catering to every whimsical mood and occasion. But most importantly, it is so often a way of making the best of whatever ingredients we have to hand.

This is not to say it is a vehicle for using up odds and ends, although on occasions you can achieve very fine results by marrying whatever you have in the fridge. Countless soups in this book have been born of an enjoyable early evening hour spent hovering over the stove, adding, tasting, simmering, adding and tasting. But never should this involve 'bits of this and bits of that' which are past their best; fill a pot with second-rate ingredients and you will get a second-rate soup. The one exception to the rule is a vegetable that has a good flavour but a poor texture, that will make an excellent creamed soup once it has been puréed and sieved. But if the flavour isn't there in the first place, you won't turn water into wine.

Any economy of means lies with the soup cycle as it were, the way it fits into our weekly repertoire. For any household who settles to roast chicken or guinea fowl on a regular basis, it is good husbandry to take it to its logical conclusion and simmer up a pot of stock at the end. Slightly stale bread can also be turned into a virtue, something not lost on French patisseries where the faintly burned or day-old loaves are sold in a basket labelled as '*pain au soupe*', for crumbling into a *pot au feu* or a *poule au pot* to eke it out. But aside from such parsimony, a beautiful soup begins with beautiful ingredients.

This doesn't necessarily mean expensive. Soups based on lentils and beans, and pot vegetables such as carrots, celery and onions, have humble roots. But others such as fish soups, and ones containing lots of cheese or a large amount of herbs will be among the most luxurious dishes you can devise. Either way, the starting point is to go shopping.

I am showing my age when I reminisce that shopping for food as a child meant a stroll down a parade of shops, a trip in turn to the greengrocer, the butcher, the fishmonger, the baker and that near extinct shop, the grocer, with its shelves stacked with artfully packaged dried beans, lentils and rice, spices and flour. Even though such shopping today is the stuff of week-end jaunts and holidays when there is the time to indulge, I still map out what I am going to buy in this way.

Aside from the quality of the produce, the experience itself is so pleasurable. Being able to look at ingredients, to admire the way they are displayed and packaged, seeking advice from those selling them or inspiration on how to cook them, generally engaging with someone with the produce at the centre, is a precursor to cooking it.

Introduction

Hence the chapters that follow evoke a stroll down a traditional high street, each shop doing what it does best. Most soups will contain a selection of ingredients, but for every one there is normally a single ingredient at its heart that relates to one particular shop – be it leeks from the greengrocer for a *potage parmentier*, some mussels from the fishmonger for a *moules marinière* or a hunk of mature farmhouse Cheddar for a cauliflower cheese soup. And I believe if you approach soups in this way, centring them on one fine ingredient and letting that lead, rather than as a way of using up unwanted odds and ends, then you will create something special.

There is always an element of fashion within cooking, and soups mirror this more than many other foods. Aside from approaching them from a different angle to our forebears for whom they were most often a means of parsimony, there has been a broadening out in our perception of soup in recent years.

Traditionally soups were either thin, creamed or consommés, whereas today they embrace all manner of dishes that are halfway to being stews. I adore these kind of soups, a mass of vegetables and snippets of meat, often with lots of extra virgin olive oil and chopped herbs.

The dividing line between 'is it or isn't it a soup?', is for me whether or not you would ladle it over buttery spuds or rice. If, despite its heartiness, you would eat it with a spoon and some bread on the side, then in my eyes it qualifies as a soup. So many of the recipes in this book, and in particular in the butcher and fishmonger chapters, are the stuff of main courses. There are also classic creamed or puréed soups, and others that broaden out the perception – a jellied red pepper and tequila soup for instance, which can be eaten scooped onto fine slivers of toast, or a French onion soup baked in the oven, that is something like a savoury bread pudding.

I am more inclined to afford soup the star role with some cheese to follow than to make it the first course. And it fits so well into family life – my love of soups was kindled with the advent of young children who are inveterate 'dippers'. They love nothing more than dunking a piece of bread into soup, a great way of deceiving them into eating all manner of nutritious vegetables they might otherwise turn their noses up at. It's an excuse for a trip to the baker for a well-crafted rustic loaf that succeeds in being moist and chewy at the same time, with a crust that invites your teeth to grip and tear it apart. In a perfect world it will have been baked in a wood-fired oven, its base cast with a pale greeny-grey bloom of ashes, which all adds to the flavour. Treat yourself to a particularly fine loaf or two, with rosemary, olives or garlic, sunflower seeds and spelt, or walnuts, or a loaf that includes potato or maize, or a sourdough bread, all of which add to the general *joie de vivre* of a large warming bowlful.

I also love dressing soups up, whether it's a fried crouton swiped with a clove of garlic in the bottom of the bowl to soak it up, or a spoon of crème fraîche mashed with Roquefort cheese that melts into it. So there are lots of suggestions for little asides and frills in what follows, but few are essential and if all you are after is a really simple bowlful, then these can be left out. But otherwise, hidden treasures and surprises add to the interest, and that most comforting of meals, a soup supper.

The Greengrocer

Of all the shops along the high street, it is the greengrocer I find most alluring, with its damp musty scent of earth clinging to roots and crates piled precariously high. A good greengrocer is an extension of a market garden, at any time of year a window onto the season, a reminder of what is at its best and what we should be enjoying at that particular time. There is hardly a vegetable that won't shine in a soup given the chance — a medium that takes what is fine and runs with it. We may not readily warm to the do-good austerity of raw vegetables, but soups play to their soft side — and encapsulate everything that we love about them in liquid comfort form.

Tomato consommé

Serves 4 1.5kg ripe plum tomatoes, halved
½ teaspoon sea salt

½ teaspoon caster sugar
4 small basil leaves (optional), to serve

Place the tomatoes in a large saucepan, cover with a lid and heat very gently for 30–40 minutes until soft, stirring occasionally. Line a sieve with a tea towel or with muslin, set it over a bowl containing the salt and sugar and tip in the tomatoes and juice. Leave for a good hour, ideally overnight, so that as much of the juice as possible runs through.

Once you are ready to serve, stir the soup, taste for seasoning and reheat gently, or serve cold. Spoon into small cups and float a basil leaf on the surface of each cup if you wish. Accompany with the bruschettas (see below) and a radish salad on the side (see page 13) if you wish.

On the side ## Bruschetta with butter bean purée and cavolo nero

These are as butch as the consommé is feint, so they make a good contrast. As well as cavolo nero, ruby chard is another contender, but step up the quantity by about half and cook it for a few minutes less.

200g cavolo nero, tough stalks cut out, washed
6 tablespoons extra virgin olive oil, plus
extra to serve
sea salt

½ lemon
1 x 400g tin of butter beans, drained and rinsed
1 garlic clove, peeled and coarsely chopped
8 slices of baguette, 1cm thick

Bring a large pan of salted water to the boil, add the cavolo nero and boil for 10 minutes. Drain into a sieve and press out any excess liquid using a large spoon. Remove to a chopping board and slice, and then place in a bowl. Dress with 2 tablespoons olive oil, a little salt and a squeeze of lemon juice. Leave to cool.

Place the butter beans in a food processor with the garlic, 4 tablespoons olive oil and some salt and whizz to a purée. Add the remaining lemon juice to taste.

To serve the bruschettas, toast the slices of baguette – you may find it easier to do this under the grill than in a toaster. Lay the slices of toast out on a large plate, drizzle over a little oil, and then place a heaped teaspoon of the butter bean purée on top. Top with a heaped teaspoon of the greens and drizzle over a little more oil.

This renders a tiny cup of crystal clear consommé — beauty before quantity. It is no more than the juice from fresh tomatoes, seasoned to bring out their flavour, so the only thing that really matters is the quality of that one ingredient. The rest of the tomato needn't go to waste, however, you can press the pulp through a sieve and use it in a sauce.

Summer's day courgette soup

If we can choose the stage set, then transport yourself to a hot, dusty city in southern Italy in the middle of summer. You chance across a backstreet restaurant with a couple of tables in the shade, with a limited menu, but most alluring a bowl of chunky vegetable soup made early that morning, that has reached an ambient temperature come your arrival at lunchtime, scarcely cool. There is something about vegetable soups such as minestrone eaten at this temperature that combine the freshness of being newly cooked, with an added flavour and sweetness that intensifies on cooling. Frying the courgettes until they are golden brings out their delicacy and succulence, and laced with basil purée makes for a rich spoonful. Back to reality, it is still very good chilled down.

Serves 6

120ml extra virgin olive oil, plus extra
*   for frying the courgettes*
1.5kg courgettes, ends removed, quartered
*   lengthways and sliced*
sea salt, black pepper

5 garlic cloves, peeled and finely chopped
1 litre vegetable stock
50g basil leaves
a couple of squeezes of lemon juice

You will need to cook the courgettes in batches. Heat a couple of tablespoons of olive oil in a large saucepan over a medium heat, add about a third of the courgettes, season and fry for 10–15 minutes until meltingly tender and golden. Cook the rest in the same way, stirring in the garlic a couple of minutes before the end. You will find the batches colour more quickly as you go on.

Return all the courgettes to the pan, add the stock and season generously with salt. Bring to the boil and then remove from the heat. Whizz half of the soup in a food processor, and then stir it back into the pan with the rest of the soup. Pour into a bowl and leave to cool.

Meanwhile, whizz the basil with 120ml olive oil in a food processor to give you a textured purée. Stir half the basil purée into the soup and season to taste with lemon juice. Ladle the soup into bowls and serve the rest of the purée spooned over.

The Greengrocer

Chilled avocado soup

I have never been comfortable with the word 'smoothie', but I guess this soup is closely affiliated – a whizzed up chilled soup, silky and pale green. The cucumber takes the place of stock here, which is more in keeping with the temperature. And to its credit, unlike many avocado soups that edge their way to a sludgy brown after an hour or so, this will be good for a day.

Serves 4

2 avocados, halved

3 cucumbers, ends discarded, peeled and cut into pieces

2 shallots, peeled and roughly chopped

1 tablespoon cider vinegar

3 tablespoons extra virgin olive oil, plus extra to serve

sea salt, black pepper

a shake of Tabasco

a few slivers of spring onion

Scoop the avocado flesh into a liquidiser, add all the remaining ingredients except the spring onion and blend until smooth. Transfer to a bowl, and then cover and chill for a couple of hours. The soup should be eaten on the day it's made. Serve with a drizzle of oil and a few slivers of spring onion. Accompany with smoked salmon and a little radish salad on the side (see below) if you wish.

On the side

Smoked salmon

black pepper

125–150g sliced smoked salmon, cut into wide strips

lemon wedges, to serve

Grind some black pepper over the smoked salmon and serve with the lemon wedges.

Radish salad

150g breakfast radishes, trimmed and thinly sliced

2 tablespoons mayonnaise

sea salt

6 tablespoons alfalfa sprouts

Mix the radishes with the mayonnaise in a bowl and season to taste with salt. Place a tablespoon of alfalfa sprouts on four plates, spreading them out a little. Spoon the radish salad on top and scatter with a few more sprouts.

Jellied red pepper and tequila soup

A soup that crosses a divide into the realms of mousses and patés. This is just as good spooned onto rice crackers, or scooped up with thin toast as it is eaten with a spoon. And it's light to boot.

Serves 6

4–5 tablespoons extra virgin olive oil

2 medium onions, peeled and chopped

3 garlic cloves, peeled and finely chopped

900g red peppers, core and seeds removed, coarsely chopped

200g ripe tomatoes, quartered

1 bay leaf

sea salt

5 sheets of gelatine (i.e. Super Cook), cut into broad strips

2 tablespoons tequila

a squeeze of lime juice

To serve

fromage frais or Greek yogurt

a few brightly coloured petals (e.g. marigold, nasturtium, clover, rose, etc.)

Heat a couple of tablespoons of oil in a large frying pan over a medium heat, add the onions and fry for about 5 minutes until softened and starting to colour, stirring occasionally. Stir in the garlic and fry for a minute or so, and then transfer everything to a large saucepan and set aside.

You will need to cook the peppers in batches. Add another couple of tablespoons of oil to the frying pan, and fry a half or one-third of the peppers for 6–8 minutes until coloured in patches, stirring occasionally. Transfer these to the saucepan with the onions, leaving behind the oil. Fry the rest of the peppers in the same way, adding more oil as necessary, and then place them in the saucepan.

Add the tomatoes, bay leaf, 200ml water and some salt to the saucepan. Bring to the boil, and then cover and cook over a low heat for 20 minutes. Towards the end of this time, place the gelatine strips in a bowl, cover with cold water and soak for 5 minutes, and then drain.

Discarding the bay leaf, purée the vegetables and juices in a liquidiser and pass through a sieve. You should have about 900ml of purée. Spoon some of this over the soaked gelatine and stir to dissolve, and then add this back into the rest of the purée. Stir in the tequila and the lime juice and add more salt if necessary. Divide the soup between six 150ml ramekins or other little cups or bowls. Place in a dish or on a tray for ease of transporting them, and then cover and leave to cool. Chill in the fridge overnight. Serve with a teaspoon of fromage frais or Greek yogurt in the centre, and a few petals strewn over.

Vichyssoise

The reputation of this soup precedes it, and since it consists of round about a third cream, I guess it should slip down a treat. A variation is to make it with spring onions (about 300g), trimmed and sliced.

It is readily dressed up and especially good with a little smoked salmon, some prawns and the like, as well as these crab toasts.

Serves 6

450g potatoes (maincrop or waxy),
  peeled and roughly diced
50g unsalted butter
280g white of leek, sliced
2 sticks of celery heart, sliced

150ml white wine
850ml chicken stock
sea salt, white pepper
300ml single cream
finely chopped chives, to serve

Bring a pan of salted water to the boil and cook the potatoes until tender. Drain and press them through a sieve. Melt the butter in a large saucepan and fry the leek and celery over a very low heat for 12–15 minutes, stirring frequently to prevent them colouring. Add the wine and cook to reduce it. Then add the chicken stock and some seasoning. Bring to the boil, and then cover and simmer over a low heat for 20 minutes. Liquidise the soup and whisk in the puréed potato. Pass through a fine-mesh sieve, stir in the cream and taste for seasoning.

To serve hot, gently reheat the soup without boiling and ladle into warm bowls. Scatter some chives over each bowl and serve with the crab toasts (see below) if you wish. Alternatively, serve it lightly chilled.

On the side

Crab toasts

Crab is a shellfish that can be prohibitively expensive. It is the brown meat that has the most flavour, something that Shippam's have long made a virtue of with their pots of spread, which can be eked out into a silky little pâté with lots of butter.

2 x 75g jars of crab paste or spread,
  e.g. Shippam's
80g unsalted butter, softened
a squeeze or two of lemon juice

a shake of Tabasco
sea salt
thin slices of baguette, toasted

Whizz the crab paste, butter, lemon juice, Tabasco and a little salt in a food processor until smooth. Dollop onto slices of toasted baguette.

Leek and potato soup

This is a country cousin of *vichyssoise*, but without the cream you can settle down to a serious bowlful followed by another. I crave this soup whenever I am feeling below par, and am happy to live off it for many days at a time. There is something about the sweetness of the leeks with the comforting nibs of potatoes. The bacon is a frill, and for the most part I am happy to pass on this bit, but it's good to know how to adorn your bowl of soup should you wish.

Serves 6

50g unsalted butter
700g leeks (trimmed weight), sliced
1 large onion, peeled and chopped
200ml white wine
1.3 litres fresh chicken or vegetable stock

170g maincrop potatoes, peeled and thinly sliced
sea salt, black pepper
To serve
200g rindless unsmoked streaky bacon, diced
snipped chives

Melt the butter in a large saucepan over a medium-low heat and fry the leeks and onion for 8–10 minutes until silky and soft, without colouring, stirring occasionally. Add the wine and reduce until syrupy. Meanwhile, bring the stock to the boil in a separate pan. Add the sliced potatoes to the leeks and stir them around for a minute, then pour the boiling stock over. Season and simmer for 8 minutes. At the same time, heat a dry frying pan over a medium-low heat, add the bacon and fry for 7–8 minutes until dark and crisp, stirring occasionally. Remove with a slotted spoon to a bowl and set aside.

Blitz the soup in batches in a food processor to a textured slurry. Return to a clean saucepan, taste to check the seasoning and reheat gently. Ladle the soup into warm bowls, scatter over some bacon and chives and serve.

Potage parmentier

Asked on the spot to name a favourite food writer I am always at a loss, and then the answer or some thoughts on the subject trickle through in the hours that follow. 'I meant to say Patricia Wells,' I suddenly recall, a cookery writer whose recipes are always superb and whose writing is beautifully evocative. Patricia Wells tells of her love of *potage parmentier* in her book *Bistro Cooking.* I'm not sure anyone else could convince me that a soup consisting of mainly potatoes, a couple of leeks and crème fraîche could be anything short of lacking – but it is every bit as good as she says.

Serves 6

500g potatoes (maincrop or waxy), peeled and
    roughly diced
2 good-sized leeks, trimmed and sliced

sea salt, black pepper
180g crème fraîche
finely chopped tarragon or chervil, to serve

Place the vegetables, 1 litre water and some seasoning in a medium saucepan. Bring to the boil, and then simmer over a low heat for 30 minutes. Purée in a liquidiser, return to the saucepan and stir in the crème fraîche. Reheat and serve scattered with herbs.

Chunky pea soup

Serves 4

5 tablespoons extra virgin olive oil, plus extra to serve
5 shallots, peeled, halved and thinly sliced
1 celery heart, trimmed and thinly sliced
3 garlic cloves, peeled and finely chopped
5 leeks, trimmed, halved lengthways and thinly sliced

sea salt, black pepper
300g fresh shelled peas
900ml chicken stock
100g pea shoots, coarsely chopped, plus a few extra shoots to serve
3 large handfuls of basil leaves

Heat 5 tablespoons of olive oil in a large saucepan over a medium heat, add the shallots, celery and garlic and cook for 4–5 minutes until softened and relaxed, stirring frequently. Add the leeks, season and cook for 4–5 minutes until glossy and relaxed, stirring occasionally. Stir in the peas, add the stock and bring to the boil, and then simmer for 5 minutes. Stir in the chopped pea shoots and cook for a further minute. Transfer half the soup to a food processor, add the basil and whizz to a textured purée, then stir this back into the pan with the rest of the soup. Taste for seasoning. Serve with a sprig of pea shoots in the middle of each bowl and plenty of olive oil drizzled over.

Wild garlic soup

Great for soothing frazzled nerves, this has lots of potato, and a mass of chopped wild garlic added at the end – something we are surrounded by in Normandy, and one of the special treats during our Easter holidays there. The small white garlic petals can be scattered over the soup, a little like chive flowers, at the end. This is great made with watercress, rocket and pea shoots too.

Serves 4–6

50g unsalted butter
4 medium onions, peeled and chopped quite finely
225ml white wine
700g potatoes (maincrop or waxy), peeled and roughly diced

1.2 litres chicken stock
sea salt, black pepper
200g wild garlic leaves, plus a few flowers, (optional), to serve
crème fraîche (optional), to serve

Melt the butter in a large saucepan over a medium-low heat, add the onions and fry for 6–7 minutes until soft and glossy, without colouring. Add the wine, turn up the heat, bring to the boil and reduce by two-thirds. Add the potatoes, the chicken stock and some seasoning, and bring back to the boil. Turn the heat back down and simmer for 15 minutes or until the potatoes are tender when pierced with a knife. Using a potato masher, coarsely mash the potatoes into the soup. It needn't be completely smooth, small nibs of potato are welcome. You can prepare the soup to this point in advance.

Just before eating, thinly slice the wild garlic and add it to the pan. Bring back to the boil and taste for seasoning. Ladle into warm soup bowls and serve straight away. You might like to drop a teaspoon of crème fraîche into the centre of each bowl of steaming soup and scatter over a few wild garlic flowers if you have some.

This chunky pea soup makes the most of their comforting sweetness, with lots of pea shoots thrown in at the very end to provide a lively note. A little grated Parmesan would be very welcome here.

As you can't have failed to notice, I love texture in soups — something a little more challenging and interesting than a simple creamed soup, lovely as these are on occasions. This is especially true when soup is supper in itself, as it makes me feel as though I've eaten properly. Here not only do the broccoli stalks come up trumps once they've been whizzed in a food processor, but almonds too bring a textured something to the party.

Broccoli and almond soup

Serves 6

500g broccoli
25g unsalted butter
1 tablespoon extra virgin olive oil
1 large onion, peeled, halved and sliced
1 celery heart, trimmed and sliced

50g flaked almonds
1.4 litres chicken stock
150ml white wine
sea salt, black pepper
fromage frais (optional), to serve

Trim and finely slice the broccoli stalks, then cut up the florets. Heat the butter and oil in a large saucepan over a medium heat, add the onion, celery, broccoli stalks and almonds and fry for 10 minutes, stirring occasionally, until softened and lightly coloured. Meanwhile, bring the stock to the boil in a small saucepan.

Add the wine to the vegetables and cook until syrupy and reduced. Add the broccoli florets and stir for a moment until they darken, then pour over the stock, which should come back to the boil almost instantly. Season the soup and simmer for 5 minutes, and then purée it in a food processor. It should retain a slight texture, specked with the green of the broccoli. Taste for seasoning and serve in warm bowls with a spoon of fromage frais in the centre if wished.

Broad bean soup with basil

In theory 150g of bacon will do nicely for the crispy lardons, but I find wandering fingers tend to dispense with a considerable proportion before they hit the soup, and 250g can be a better bet. Remember if buying a ready-made stock or powder that it may already contain salt, so to season the soup at the end.

Serves 4

40g unsalted butter
2 medium onions, peeled and chopped
2 garlic cloves, peeled and finely chopped
1 celery heart, trimmed and sliced
150ml white wine
750g frozen broad beans
1 litre chicken or vegetable stock

sea salt, black pepper
2 large handfuls of basil leaves
To serve
150g smoked lardons (or rindless streaky
    bacon, diced)
crème fraîche (optional), to serve

Melt the butter in a medium saucepan over a medium heat, add the onion, garlic and celery and fry gently for 8–10 minutes until softened and starting to colour. Add the wine and simmer until well-reduced and syrupy. Add the broad beans and the stock, bring to the boil and simmer for about 7 minutes. Liquidise the soup in batches with the basil, then pass it through a sieve back into a clean pan and taste for seasoning.

While the soup is cooking, gently fry the lardons (or diced bacon) in a dry frying pan over a medium-low heat, stirring frequently until golden and crisp. Drain on kitchen paper. Reheat the soup, and serve in warm bowls with a dollop of crème fraîche in the centre if you wish, and some lardons scattered over. Both the soup and the lardons can be made in advance – you may need to gently reheat the lardons if the fat has set.

Favourite tomato soup

This is a fresh take on Heinz, the variety so many of us crave, having been spoonfed this velvety red soup, with lots of melted cheese if we were lucky, when our mothers were too busy for anything else. For best results, go for cherry tomatoes on the vine, which are the sweetest and most intensely flavoured tomatoes of all. But the real secret here is the celery salt, and it's well worth investing in a jar, although failing that you could sauté a couple of sticks of sliced celery heart with the onions.

Serves 6

50g unsalted butter

2 medium onions, peeled and chopped

4 garlic cloves, peeled and finely chopped

1.5kg ripe cherry tomatoes (or plum tomatoes, coarsely chopped)

150ml whipping cream

¾ teaspoon caster sugar

sea salt

cayenne pepper

celery salt

Melt the butter in a large saucepan over a lowish heat and fry the onion for about 10 minutes until lightly coloured, stirring occasionally. Add the garlic a couple of minutes before the end. Add the tomatoes and give them a quick stir, and then cover the pan with a lid and cook for 20–25 minutes until the tomatoes are soft and soupy, stirring halfway through.

Purée the soup in a liquidiser and pass through a sieve. Return to a clean pan, add the cream, sugar and a little salt, and simmer gently for 15 minutes. Season with cayenne pepper and celery salt to taste.

Tinned tomato soup

While Andy Warhol was busy turning Campbell's tomato soup cans into icons, it's a shame he didn't explore the other brands – Heinz is streets ahead. To sex it up try it:

~ *with a spoonful of fresh pesto*

~ *with a dollop of crème fraîche and some croutons*

~ *liquidised with some fresh basil*

~ *ladled over a slice of toast drizzled with olive oil and scattered with plenty of chopped flat-leaf parsley*

~ *with lots of grated smoked Cheddar, such as Applewood*

~ *with little toasts piled with fried onions, scattered with Gruyère and grilled*

~ *with flakes of cooked smoked haddock and diced potato stirred in, scattered with snipped chives or flat-leaf parsley – an instant chowder*

Tomato cup-a-soup

This is for when you want a real, but instant, tomato soup. Drink it from mugs with a few croutons for a bit of crunch.

Serves 4–6

150ml single cream
150ml milk
1 medium onion, peeled and quartered
1 stick of celery heart, trimmed and sliced
1 medium carrot, trimmed, peeled and sliced
2 x 400g tins of chopped tomatoes

1 tablespoon tomato ketchup
pinch of cayenne pepper
1 teaspoon cornflour
1 heaped teaspoon caster sugar
sea salt
croutons (optional), to serve

Combine the cream and milk in a medium saucepan. Whizz all the remaining ingredients in a blender and add to the pan. Bring to the boil and simmer for 15 minutes, stirring occasionally. Serve with a scattering of croutons (see page 165) if you wish.

Butternut squash soup with nutmeg and ginger

Butternut squash promises a more intense soup than pumpkin, and it tends to be my default when I am hovering between the two. But equally I love experimenting with different types of squash, and enjoy buying pumpkin by the slice when I come across it sold in that fashion, which is quite usual in Normandy. For this recipe the two are interchangeable.

Serves 6

Croutons

groundnut or vegetable oil, for shallow-frying

3 thin slices of white bread, crusts removed, diced

Soup

50g unsalted butter

1 large onion, peeled and chopped

2 tablespoons coarsely chopped fresh root ginger

2 x 900g butternut squash, skinned, deseeded and coarsely chopped*

1 litre fresh vegetable or chicken stock

sea salt, black pepper

150g crème fraîche

freshly grated nutmeg

To make the croutons, heat a few millimetres of oil in a large frying pan over a medium heat until a cube of bread is immersed in bubbles when added to the pan. Put in the bread cubes and fry until golden, stirring frequently. Remove, drain on double-thickness kitchen paper and leave to cool.

To make the soup, melt the butter in a large saucepan over a medium heat, add the onion, ginger and squash and fry for about 5 minutes until glossy, stirring frequently. Add the stock and plenty of seasoning and bring to the boil, pressing the squash down with a spoon to submerge it. Simmer for 5–10 minutes until the squash is tender. Liquidise the soup in batches in a blender along with the crème fraîche and a generous grating of nutmeg, then pass it through a sieve. Gently reheat, and serve scattered with croutons.

* The simplest route here is to cut off a slice from the top and the bottom of the butternut squash and halve it where the bulb meets the trunk. Cut the skin off both sections, and then quarter, deseed and slice the bulb, and halve and slice the trunk.

Spinach soup with ricotta

A real pond green, not that I say that affectionately ever since a blanket of pond weed smothered my wild watercress, but it is a fabulous colour, and the milky whiteness of the ricotta makes it even more dramatic. Gently warmed by the heat of the soup, the cheese is rendered exquisitely soft and creamy – in contrast to the crispness of the bacon.

Serves 4

50g unsalted butter
3 medium onions (ideally white), peeled and chopped
sea salt, black pepper
150ml white wine
1 litre chicken stock
500g spinach
80g curly or flat-leaf parsley (leaves and fine stalks)
a squeeze of lemon juice
To serve
8 rashers rindless smoked streaky bacon
4 tablespoons ricotta

Melt the butter in a large saucepan over a lowish heat, add the onions, scatter over a teaspoon of salt and fry for 15–20 minutes until soft and syrupy, stirring occasionally, without allowing them to colour. Add the wine, turn the heat up and cook to reduce it by half. Pour in the chicken stock and bring to the boil. Put in the spinach with half the parsley, bring back to the boil, and then cover and cook over a low heat for 10 minutes, stirring the soup after a couple of minutes to submerge the leaves. Add the remaining parsley at the last minute, and then purée the soup in a liquidiser. Season with black pepper and a little more salt if necessary.

Gently reheat the soup, and add a squeeze of lemon juice – if this is added too far in advance the soup will dull in colour.

While the soup is cooking, heat the grill and cook the bacon on both sides until golden and crisp. Place a tablespoon of ricotta in the centre of four warm soup bowls and ladle the soup around it. Lay a couple of rashers of bacon in the middle and serve straight away.

Sweetcorn and chilli soup

Serves 6

30g unsalted butter
2 tablespoons extra virgin olive oil
2 large onions, peeled and finely chopped
7 corn cobs
3 teaspoons finely chopped medium-hot
*   red chilli*

1 litre vegetable stock
sea salt
2 tablespoons lemon juice
5 tablespoons coarsely chopped flat-leaf parsley,
*   plus extra to serve*
soured cream (optional), to serve

Heat the butter and olive oil in a large saucepan over a medium heat and fry the onion for about 10 minutes until nice and golden, stirring occasionally. Meanwhile, strip the kernels off the cobs using a sharp knife. Add these to the pan with the chilli and fry for about 5 minutes, stirring occasionally. Add the stock and some salt, bring to the boil and simmer for 10 minutes until the corn is tender, but still crisp. Transfer two-thirds of the soup to a food processor and whizz to a coarse purée. Add this back to the pan and stir in the lemon juice and parsley. Taste for seasoning. Serve with a spoonful of soured cream if you wish, and some more parsley scattered over.

Celeriac and grainy mustard soup

Celery has a very distinctive flavour, that acquires an added dimension when combined with its relative celeriac, which gives the soup a thick wholesome texture – whereas celery on its own is all water.

You could enrich the finished soup with some cream if you wish, or serve it with a swirl on top before scattering over the bacon and pine nuts.

Serves 6

70g unsalted butter
2 leeks, trimmed and sliced
2 celery hearts, trimmed and sliced
*   (inner leaves reserved)*
800g celeriac, peeled and chopped
sea salt, white pepper

1 litre chicken or vegetable stock
1 teaspoon grainy mustard
To serve
150g rindless smoked streaky bacon, diced
50g pine nuts

Melt the butter in a large saucepan over a low heat. Add the leeks, celery and celeriac, sprinkle over a heaped teaspoon of sea salt and fry very gently for 30 minutes, stirring frequently to prevent the vegetables from colouring. Add the stock, bring to the boil and simmer over a low heat for 15 minutes. Purée the soup in batches in a liquidiser, and then pass through a sieve back into the pan. Whisk in the mustard and taste to check the seasoning.

At the same time, heat the bacon in a large frying pan over a medium heat and fry in the rendered fat, stirring occasionally until golden and crisp. Add the pine nuts towards the end and fry for a couple of minutes. Drain on double-thickness kitchen paper.

Gently reheat the soup and ladle into warm bowls. Scatter the bacon over the top and garnish with a few chopped celery leaves.

The idea of stripping kernels from a cob immediately smacks of life's-too-short-to-stuff-a-mushroom, when in truth it takes no time at all – providing you take care not to let them shoot all over the kitchen worksurfaces and floor. The soup is true to its name, really sweet, but sharpened with a little lemon juice so it is well balanced.

Chunky carrot, saffron and coriander soup

There is method in the apparent madness of this soup. Trust me that the end result is transformed by glazing the carrots first so that they take on an intense buttery sweetness, which is subsequently transferred to the saffron broth.

Serves 6

1.2kg large carrots, trimmed and peeled
3 shallots, peeled and finely chopped
1 litre chicken or vegetable stock
60g unsalted butter, diced
large pinch of saffron filaments (about 30)
1 heaped teaspoon sea salt
1 heaped teaspoon caster sugar
150g crème fraîche
6 tablespoons chopped coriander, plus a little extra to serve

Quarter the carrots lengthways and finely slice – you can do this with the slicing attachment of a food processor. Place them in a large saucepan with the shallots, 200ml stock, the butter, saffron, salt and sugar. Give everything a stir, bring the liquid to a simmer, and then cover and cook over a medium heat for 8 minutes. Give the carrots another stir, turn up the heat and cook, uncovered, for 8–12 minutes, stirring towards the end to stop them from catching. You will know when they are ready because the stock will have evaporated and the carrots will be glossy, coated in a buttery emulsion and meltingly tender.

Add the remaining stock and the crème fraîche and bring to the boil, and then stir in the chopped coriander and season with more salt if necessary. Serve the soup in shallow bowls with the carrots piled in the centre, and a little more coriander scattered over the top.

Cauliflower and coriander soup

I am always amazed that with so few ingredients this soup can still pack such a punch, it's gorgeously aromatic, creamy white and silky. A coriander purée, stirred through at the end, lifts it a treat.

Serves 4

30g unsalted butter
1 onion, peeled and chopped
1 small cauliflower, cut into small florets
(about 600g)
100ml white wine

sea salt, white pepper
To serve
20g coriander leaves
3 tablespoons extra virgin olive oil
a squeeze of lemon juice

Melt the butter in a large saucepan over a medium-low heat. Add the onion, cauliflower and wine and cook for 10–15 minutes, stirring occasionally, until the cauliflower changes from a chalky white to a translucent white, without colouring. Add 700ml water, plenty of salt and a little pepper. Bring to the boil, and then cover and cook over a low heat for 15 minutes. Purée in a blender and return to the saucepan.

Meanwhile, whizz the coriander, olive oil, lemon juice and a pinch of salt in a food processor to a purée. Serve the soup with a spoonful of the herb purée drizzled over. Accompany with Skinny beef and Coleslaw (see below) if you wish.

On the side

Skinny beef

300g piece of beef fillet
extra virgin olive oil

sea salt, black pepper

Remove the beef from the fridge 20 minutes before cooking. Heat a frying pan over a medium-high heat. Brush the fillet all over with oil and season. Sear the beef for 3–4 minutes on all four sides until it feels springy but soft, which will leave it medium-rare. Place it on a rack set over a plate, loosely cover with foil and leave to cool, then wrap it in the foil and chill for at least an hour. Finely slice to serve.

Coleslaw

3 tablespoons soured cream
a couple of squeezes of lemon juice
sea salt, cayenne pepper
1/8 onion
1/3 Savoy cabbage, heart only, finely sliced

1 slim carrot, trimmed, peeled and finely sliced
on the diagonal
1/4 apple, cored and finely sliced
a handful of watercress
2 tablespoons walnut oil
30g macadamia nuts

Blend the soured cream with a squeeze of lemon juice, a little salt and the juice from the onion, squeezing it with a garlic press. Arrange the cabbage, carrot, apple and watercress on a plate. Drizzle over the walnut oil and a squeeze of lemon juice, and scrunch over a little salt. Spoon the soured cream dressing over the top, dust with cayenne pepper and scatter with the macadamias.

Two-pepper soup

A smooth, thick red soup with the warming heat of chilli, and a little ginger. Chicken kebabs and a broccoli salad turn it into a more substantial supper.

Serves 4

4–5 tablespoons groundnut oil

1kg red peppers, core and seeds removed, coarsely chopped

2 medium onions, peeled and coarsely chopped

3 medium carrots, trimmed, peeled and sliced

1 celery heart, trimmed and sliced

3 garlic cloves, peeled and finely chopped

1 scant teaspoon finely chopped medium-hot red chilli

1 teaspoon coarsely chopped fresh root ginger

2 ripe tomatoes, halved

150ml white wine

sea salt

pinch of caster sugar

4 pickled piri-piri peppers (or other small pickled chillies), to serve

You will need to cook the peppers in batches. Heat a couple of tablespoons of oil in a large saucepan over a medium heat, add half the peppers and fry for 8–10 minutes until lightly coloured, glossy and relaxed, stirring occasionally. Transfer to a bowl while you cook the rest in the same way, adding another tablespoon of oil if necessary. Keep to one side.

Add another couple of tablespoons of oil to the pan, put in the onion, carrot and celery and fry for about 5 minutes until softened and starting to colour, stirring occasionally. Stir in the garlic, chilli and ginger and cook for a few minutes to release their flavour. Add the tomatoes and the wine and cook until well-reduced. Add the peppers back to the pan, pour in 400ml water and season with a generous dose of salt and the sugar. Bring to the boil, and then cover and cook over a low heat for 10 minutes. Liquidise the soup and pass it through a sieve, and then taste for seasoning. Ladle into warm bowls and serve with a pickled piri-piri pepper in the centre. Accompany with five-spice chicken sticks and a broccoli and sesame seed salad if you wish (see right).

Five-spice chicken sticks

Five-spice is a great blend that calls for little else in a marinade for chicken. The smell as the sticks grill is tantalisingly good.

> *2 skinless free-range chicken breasts*
> *groundnut or vegetable oil*
> *1 scant teaspoon five-spice powder*
> *2 garlic cloves, peeled and crushed to a paste*
> *1 medium red onion, peeled*
> *sea salt, black pepper*
> *lime wedges, to serve*

Cut the chicken into 2–3cm cubes and toss in a bowl with a tablespoon of oil, the five-spice powder and the garlic. Cover and chill for at least one hour. Cut the onion into chunks the same size as the chicken. Thread the onion and chicken a couple of pieces at a time onto eight 10–12cm skewers.

Heat a large frying pan over a medium heat. Meanwhile, season the chicken kebabs and drizzle with a little oil. Grill for about 2 minutes on all four sides until golden and firm. Brush a little oil over the lime wedges and briefly fry the flesh sides to colour them.

Grilled broccoli and sesame seed salad

> *400g tender-stem broccoli, trimmed*
> *1 tablespoon sesame seeds*
> *2 tablespoons groundnut or vegetable oil*
> *2 teaspoons sesame oil*
> *sea salt, black pepper*

Bring a large pan of salted water to the boil, add the broccoli and cook for 3 minutes. Drain into a colander and leave for a few minutes for the surface moisture to evaporate before transferring to a bowl. Toast the sesame seeds in a small frying pan over a medium heat until lightly coloured, stirring constantly, and then transfer to a saucer and leave to cool.

Heat a ridged griddle over a medium heat. Blend the groundnut and sesame oils together and drizzle over the broccoli. Season with salt and pepper and toss carefully. Grill the broccoli stems in two to three batches for 2–3 minutes on each side until golden, and then arrange on a plate. Scatter over the sesame seeds and serve warm or at room temperature.

White onion soup

This is in the *vichyssoise* league of heavyweight creamed soups. Pearly white onions have a particular character and finesse, and it's quite important to use these rather than the bog-standard brown ones that are better reserved for French onion soup.

Serves 4–6

70g unsalted butter
1kg white onions, peeled, halved and sliced
3 sprigs of thyme
sea salt, white pepper

150ml white wine
700ml chicken stock
200g crème fraîche
black pepper (optional), to serve

Melt the butter in a large saucepan over a low heat. Add the onions and thyme, sprinkle over a heaped teaspoon of sea salt and fry for 30 minutes, stirring frequently to prevent the onions from colouring. By the end they should be lusciously silky and soft. Pour in the wine, turn up the heat a little and simmer until it is well-reduced. Add the chicken stock, bring to a simmer and cook over a low heat for 15 minutes.

Remove the thyme sprigs, and then purée the soup in a liquidiser along with the crème fraîche and some white pepper. Taste to check the seasoning. Return to a clean saucepan and gently reheat. Serve in warmed soup bowls and season with black pepper if wished.

Parsnip soup

Parsnips make for a fabulously aromatic soup, with the proviso that you balance their sweetness – a task performed here by the lemon juice. If you like creamy soups, you could add 150ml whipping cream at the end, or swirl a tad over the top before serving. Another tweak is the inclusion of a few rosemary or thyme sprigs along with the parsnips, removing them before you whizz the soup. The bacon and pine nuts suggested for Celeriac and grainy mustard soup (see page 30) are equally good here. This is a good one for freezing.

Serves 6

50g unsalted butter
2 medium onions, peeled and chopped
1 leek, trimmed and sliced
4 sticks of celery heart, trimmed and sliced
2 garlic cloves, peeled and finely chopped

600g parsnips, trimmed, peeled, halved
    lengthways and sliced
juice of ½ lemon
1 litre chicken or vegetable stock
sea salt, black pepper

Melt the butter in a large saucepan over a medium-low heat, add the onion, leek, celery and garlic and fry for 10–15 minutes, or until softened and glossy and just starting to colour, stirring occasionally. Add the parsnips and lemon juice and cook for 15 minutes, again stirring occasionally. Add the chicken or vegetable stock and some seasoning, bring to the boil and simmer for 10 minutes. Liquidise the soup in batches, and taste for seasoning. Serve in warmed bowls.

Beetroot and apple soup

Serves 6

80g unsalted butter
2 medium onions, peeled and chopped
2 garlic cloves, peeled and finely chopped
700g uncooked beetroot, trimmed, peeled and sliced
2 eating apples, peeled, cored and sliced

200ml dry cider
1.2 litres chicken stock
sea salt, black pepper
3 bunches spring onions, trimmed and sliced
3 tablespoons crème fraîche

Melt 50g butter in a large saucepan over a lowish heat and fry the onion and garlic for 5–8 minutes until soft and glossy, stirring occasionally. Add the beetroot and apple and continue to fry for another 5 minutes, again stirring occasionally. Add the cider and reduce until syrupy, and then add the chicken stock and some seasoning. Bring to the boil over a high heat, and then cover and simmer over a low heat for 30 minutes. Purée the soup in batches in a food processor (or liquidiser if you like a very smooth soup), and then return it to the saucepan and taste to check the seasoning.

About 10 minutes before the soup is ready, heat the remaining butter in a frying pan and fry the spring onions over a low heat until soft, about 8 minutes, seasoning them and stirring frequently.

Rewarm the soup if necessary before ladling it into warm bowls. To serve, place a spoonful of spring onions in the centre and a heaped teaspoon of crème fraîche on top. Eat straight away.

Green minestrone with mint and almond pesto

A mass of lovely late spring veggies with a mint purée coursing through the broth, this immediately evokes everything you associate with spring. Minestrone is something to be played with – basil could replace the mint and parsley, and pine nuts the almonds, which will make for a more traditional soup.

Serves 4

8 tablespoons extra virgin olive oil, plus extra
*   to serve*
1 celery heart, trimmed and sliced
2 leeks, trimmed and sliced
2 garlic cloves, peeled and finely chopped
150g French beans, ends trimmed, cut into
*   1cm pieces*
150g fresh or frozen baby broad beans

150g fresh or frozen peas
800ml vegetable stock
sea salt, black pepper
2–3 handfuls of spinach leaves
25g mint leaves
25g flat-leaf parsley leaves
25g flaked almonds
75g freshly grated Parmesan

Heat 3 tablespoons of oil in a large saucepan over a medium-low heat, add the celery and leeks and fry for 6–8 minutes until glossy and softened, stirring occasionally. Add the garlic just before the end. Stir in the French beans, broad beans and peas, and then add the stock and seasoning. Bring to the boil and simmer for 5 minutes. Add the spinach and cook for 1 minute, stirring to submerge the leaves. Whizz half the soup in a food processor to a textured purée, and then stir it back in with the rest of the soup.

Whizz the mint, parsley and almonds with 5 tablespoons of oil in a food processor, and then add the Parmesan and briefly whizz again. Stir into the hot soup right at the end and serve with a drizzle of oil.

The sweet tartness of apple brings out the flavour of beetroot. It's not a vegetable that everyone likes, it's like it or loathe it, people rarely sit on the fence with this one. But if you know you are among like-minded beetroot lovers, this is a great soup.

Double mushroom soup

This is everything I love in a mushroom soup – hearty and rustic, thick and meaty. Mushrooms are so replete with juices, they make great soup material and any variety will be good here, but the combination of chestnut and shiitake is particularly tasty, without going to the expense of wild ones.

Serves 4

5 tablespoons extra virgin olive oil, plus extra to serve

30g unsalted butter

100g unsmoked rindless streaky bacon, diced

4 shallots, peeled, halved and sliced

1 tablespoon rosemary needles

3 garlic cloves, peeled and finely chopped

1 maincrop potato (about 200g), peeled and diced

100ml white wine

400g chestnut mushrooms, trimmed and sliced

200g shiitake mushrooms, trimmed and sliced

800ml chicken or vegetable stock

¼ teaspoon dried chilli flakes

sea salt

To serve

130g shiitake mushrooms, trimmed and sliced

coarsely chopped flat-leaf parsley

Heat a tablespoon of oil and the butter in a large saucepan over a medium heat, add the bacon and fry for 4–5 minutes until starting to colour. Put in the shallot and rosemary and fry for 3 minutes, stirring in the garlic towards the end. Stir in the potato, add the wine and simmer until well-reduced and syrupy.

You will need to cook the mushrooms in batches. Heat a tablespoon of oil in a large frying pan over a high heat. Add about a third of the mushrooms and fry for a few minutes, stirring frequently, until golden. Set aside on a plate while you cook the rest in the same way.

Add the fried mushrooms to the saucepan, along with the stock, the chilli and some salt. Bring to the boil and simmer for 10 minutes. Whizz the soup in batches in a food processor and return to the pan.

To serve, heat a tablespoon of oil in a large frying pan, add the remaining 130g shiitake mushrooms, season with salt and sauté for several minutes until softened and golden. Ladle the soup into warm bowls, scatter the shiitake mushrooms over with plenty of parsley and a little drizzle of olive oil.

The Dairy

A few croutons with molten Stilton or Camembert, toasted Cheddar sandwiches, some feta stirred into a soup at the end, instantly create that comforting yummy factor that we're seeking. Or it might be a little cheese crumbled into the bowl before ladling the soup over. It's a great way of using up the ends of a slice of cheese, the darkened Stilton or hardened Cheddar inside the rind, that if anything has even more flavour than the cheese within. Such raw materials bought from a good cheese shop will be a world apart from the unloved cheese of a supermarket. It will have been 'finished' or as the French would say 'bien affiné' by someone of the same title — an affineur. The ins and outs of storing cheeses, which will depend on their type and their age, is highly specialised. I also appreciate such shops for their wider remit of untreated cream, yogurt and fromage frais, often ladled from a large tub into a smaller one on demand. There is every reason to hope such products will have just as much character as the cheeses they are next to, all of which promise rich velvety soups with limpid textures, something they make a feature of in the Middle East. You are also more likely to find products with their full complement of fat, which goes hand in hand with flavour.

Russian cherry soup

Fruit soups are an eccentricity, strikingly whimsical, and I'm not entirely sure that I can take them seriously, but the Russians do and so do the Georgians. With their enviable harvest of sour cherries, what better way of serving them than in a soup, or is it simply that fiercely cold winters drive you to frivolity come the summer?

Any scepticism I guess is mainly that they fall outside the usual remit – where does the cheeseboard and salad fit in? But therein lies the answer, they fill a gap that other soups can't. Fruit soups are at home either end of supper, and they are a fine way of preceding a spicy main course, a chicken or lamb curry perhaps, and it's not always easy to find a starter that plays to such a full-on palate. Flaky little Grecian pastries are a flight of fancy, but the singularly salty character of feta and halloumi go very well indeed.

Serves 4

75g dried cherries
2cm cinnamon stick
1 clove

*5cm strip of orange zest (removed with a
    potato peeler)*
½ bottle (375ml) sweet white wine
juice of 1 orange, strained

Place all the ingredients in a medium saucepan with 450ml water. Bring to a simmer, and then cover and cook over a low heat for 30 minutes. Discard the orange zest and pick out the spices. Leave to cool. Strain the soup through a fine mesh sieve, reserving about half of the cherries as a garnish. Cover and chill. Serve the soup in small bowls with a few cherries scattered over, accompanied by the cheese pastries (see below) if you wish. You can also serve this soup warm.

On the side

White cheese pastries

75g feta, crumbled
75g halloumi, grated
25g pine nuts
1 tablespoon chopped mint

freshly grated nutmeg
1 medium organic egg, beaten
200g filo pastry sheets
50g unsalted butter, melted

Heat the oven to 190°C fan oven/210°C electric oven. To make the filling, combine the feta and halloumi with the pine nuts, mint, some freshly grated nutmeg and the egg in a bowl.

Paint a sheet of filo pastry with a little melted butter and lay another sheet on top. Cut into rectangular strips about 7cm by 18cm. Place a heaped teaspoon of the filling near the top of one of the strips, turn in one of the long sides by 1cm, and then fold the top corner down over the filling to form a triangle. Paint the surface with a little more melted butter, and fold the parcel over and over again and again, painting the surface with each turn, until you have a small triangular package. Place this on a baking tray, and repeat with the remaining ingredients.

Liberally paint any unbuttered surfaces with butter and bake the pastries for 20 minutes until deep golden brown. Serve warm.

Pear and Stilton soup

At Christmas, the end of the Stilton can be almost more enticing than the marbled inner sanctum of lichen-tinged cheese that you enjoyed with Carr's water biscuits and slivers of celery. Inevitably the centre always gets eaten first, but the darker, stronger cheese lining the rind is not to be wasted.

Many years ago I spent New Year in a rented holiday house overlooking a Cornish beach. While the setting was spectacular, it gave new meaning to the expression 'bare essentials' in the way that only holiday homes of a certain ilk can achieve. I still remember every mouthful of the Stilton soup that we ate one evening, by far the most comforting aspect of the holiday. A rich golden turkey stock is a great match for this cheese soup, and the pears lift it discreetly without being obvious. You could serve it in little shot glasses if you're catering for any number, or simply a mixture of small coffee cups, little oriental bowls and the like, in which case it will feed many more than suggested.

Serves 4–6

50g unsalted butter
1 celery heart, trimmed and sliced
3 medium carrots, trimmed, peeled and sliced
2 leeks, trimmed and sliced
2 pears, peeled, cored and chopped
150ml white wine
900ml chicken or turkey stock

sea salt, black pepper
150g Stilton, crumbled
To serve
crème fraîche
*cocktail shortbreads (see page 167), shortbread
    nibbles or sliced baguette*

Melt the butter in a large saucepan over a medium heat, add the celery, carrot and leek and fry very gently for 8–10 minutes until glossy and softened, stirring occasionally. Add the pears and stir, then add the wine and simmer until well reduced. Add the stock and season lightly (bearing in mind the salty Stilton is still to come). Bring to the boil, and then cover and cook over a low heat for 10 minutes. Stir in the Stilton, cover and leave to stand off the heat for a few minutes to allow it to melt. Purée the soup in batches in a liquidiser, and then pass through a sieve. Taste for seasoning. Serve with a little crème fraîche dolloped in the centre, accompanied by cocktail shortbreads (see page 167), shortbread nibbles or sliced baguette.

Curried aubergine soup

Aubergine soup is an oddity perhaps, but that lovely succulence melts down a treat into a chicken stock with some spices. Here the heat is pleasantly tempered by a cooling raita.

Serves 4

6 tablespoons groundnut oil

2 medium aubergines, cut into 1cm dice

3 garlic cloves, peeled and finely chopped

2cm knob of fresh root ginger, peeled and finely chopped

1 medium-hot red chilli, seeds and membranes removed, finely sliced

½ teaspoon turmeric

1 teaspoon ground coriander

1 teaspoon ground cumin

1 litre chicken stock

sea salt

2 level teaspoons caster sugar

1 tablespoon lemon juice

4 tablespoons finely chopped coriander

warm flatbread (optional), to serve

You will need to fry the aubergine in batches. Heat 2 tablespoons oil in a large non-stick frying pan over a medium heat, add half the aubergine and fry for 7–8 minutes until soft and golden, stirring occasionally. Remove to a bowl and repeat with the remaining aubergine.

Heat 2 tablespoons oil in a medium saucepan over a medium heat, add the garlic, ginger and chilli and fry for a couple of minutes until softened and fragrant. Add the spices and stir, then add half the fried aubergine, the chicken stock, 2 teaspoons of salt and the sugar. Bring to the boil and simmer for about 8 minutes. Liquidise the soup in a blender, return to the pan and stir in the reserved aubergine. Gently reheat, and then stir in the lemon juice and fresh coriander. Taste for seasoning and serve in warm bowls. Accompany with cucumber raita (see below) and warm flatbread if wished.

On the side ## Raita

Prepare this in advance of the soup.

½ cucumber, peeled

200g fromage frais

½ teaspoon finely chopped medium-hot green chilli

pinch of caster sugar

sea salt

1 spring onion, trimmed and finely sliced

Coarsely grate the cucumber and, using your hands, squeeze out as much liquid as possible. Stir the grated cucumber into the fromage frais in a bowl, with the green chilli, sugar and a little salt to taste. Transfer to a clean serving bowl and scatter with the spring onion. You can make this up to a couple of hours in advance, in which case cover and set aside in a cool place.

Beetroot and pomegranate soup

Our fondness for beetroot pickled in vinegar is no coincidence. It is a root that relishes tart ingredients, and the most successful beetroot soups play to this – an apple in there, or a little orange juice makes all the difference. Here, though, the role is fulfilled by pomegranate, ever an artful balance of sweet and sour, it brings out the best in this curious vegetable. Their matching vermilion hues are also rather appealing.

Serves 6

50g unsalted butter
2 medium onions, peeled and chopped
700g uncooked beetroot, trimmed, peeled
*   and sliced*
2 garlic cloves, peeled and finely chopped
200ml pomegranate juice

1.2 litres fresh chicken stock
sea salt, black pepper
freshly grated nutmeg
50g pine nuts
pomegranate syrup (optional), to serve

Melt the butter in a large saucepan over a lowish heat and fry the onion for 5–8 minutes until soft and glossy, stirring occasionally. Add the beetroot and garlic and continue to fry for a further 5 minutes, again stirring occasionally. Add the pomegranate juice and reduce until syrupy, then add the chicken stock, some seasoning and a little grated nutmeg. Bring to the boil, and then cover and simmer over a low heat for 30 minutes.

Meanwhile, heat the oven to 180°C fan oven/200°C electric oven. Spread the pine nuts over the base of a small baking dish and toast for 8–9 minutes until lightly golden, then remove and leave to cool. Purée the soup in a liquidiser, and then return it to the saucepan and taste to check the seasoning. Serve the soup in warm bowls with a drizzle of pomegranate syrup if wished and a few pine nuts scattered over. It can also be accompanied with the toasties (see below).

On the side

Goat's cheese toasties

These are a little aside to the soup, if you want a whole one per person, then you'll need to double up.

6 thin slices of white bread, cut from a small loaf
100g thinly sliced hard goat's cheese

extra virgin olive oil
3 small handfuls alfalfa shoots, to serve

Make three sandwiches with the bread and sliced goat's cheese. Heat a large frying pan (ideally non-stick) over a high heat for a couple of minutes, or two pans if necessary. Add a little oil to the pan, and then add the sandwiches. Turn the heat down to medium-low and cook gently for 3–5 minutes on each side until golden on the outside and oozing melted cheese. Gently prize each one apart and fill with the alfalfa, then close and cut into quarters or fingers.

Watercress soup

I love those diminutive teasing intros to fine lunches in the form of a taster of soup sipped through a head of cream, and this soup is definitely a candidate. But it is the little toasted Cheddar sandwiches that turn it into a treat; a cheese that doesn't get enough outings given the fashionable status of so many French and Italian ones.

Serves 4–6

1.1 litres chicken or vegetable stock
50g unsalted butter
250g watercress (3 good-sized bunches), leaves and fine stalks
280g maincrop potatoes, peeled and finely sliced
sea salt, black pepper
25g flat-leaf parsley, leaves and fine stalks
crème fraîche or soured cream, to serve

Bring the stock to the boil in a small saucepan. Melt the butter in a large saucepan over a medium heat, add the watercress and stir until it wilts. Add the potato slices and cook for a minute, then pour in the boiling stock and add some seasoning. Simmer the soup for 6 minutes, then liquidise it in a blender with the parsley. Season to taste and serve with a dollop of crème fraîche or soured cream, accompanied by the toasties if you wish (see below).

On the side

Toasted Cheddar sarnies

unsalted butter for spreading
8 thin slices of white bread, cut from a small loaf
150g grated mature Cheddar
Dijon mustard

Butter the slices of bread on one side. Pair them up into sandwiches with the cheese on the inside and the butter on the outside, spreading one of the unbuttered sides in the middle with mustard. These can be made in advance, in which case cover and chill them.

To cook the sandwiches, heat a large frying pan (preferably non-stick) over a high heat for several minutes. Add as many sandwiches as will fit, turn the heat down to medium-low and cook for 4–5 minutes on each side, or until golden and the cheese has melted. Cook the rest in the same way. Cut into little squares or triangles to serve.

A classic and personal favourite. The large handful of flat-leaf parsley at the end affords it a second life and promises a leprechaun Irish green.

Celery soup with Camembert and tarragon butter

This is a soup I often cook out in Normandy where Camembert and tarragon are a given. And so too is the bread, although it need not necessarily be the finest baguette – good husbandry means that all the patisseries sell off their day-old and overcooked or slightly burnt loaves in a basket labelled 'pain au soupe'. The downside in France are those few shops that seem to burn all their bread and only have 'soupe' on offer, but as a rule of thumb it is a good system where nothing goes to waste.

Serves 4

40g unsalted butter
1 head of celery, trimmed with outer stalks
    discarded, thinly sliced
2 leeks, outer layers discarded, thinly sliced
200ml white wine
1.2 litres fresh chicken stock
sea salt, black pepper

Toasts
4 slices of baguette, 1cm thick
75g Camembert or Pont-l'Evêque, sliced

Tarragon butter
50g unsalted butter
1 heaped tablespoon chopped tarragon

Melt the butter for the soup in a large saucepan over a medium-low heat and fry the celery and leeks for 8–10 minutes until glossy and relaxed, stirring occasionally without allowing them to colour. Add the wine and reduce by half, then add the chicken stock and some seasoning. Bring to a simmer and cook over a low heat for 25 minutes.

Meanwhile, heat the oven to 200°C fan oven/220°C electric oven. Lay the slices of baguette on a baking tray and toast for 7–8 minutes until lightly coloured. Remove and leave to cool, and then lay the sliced cheese on top.

To serve, toast the croutons in the oven for 5 minutes until the cheese is melted but retains its shape. Meanwhile, melt the remaining butter and chopped tarragon together in a saucepan. Place a crouton in the base of four warmed shallow soup bowls and ladle the soup on top. Drizzle with tarragon butter and dish up straight away.

Leafy green soup with feta and olives

Serves 4

50g unsalted butter

1 celery heart, trimmed and thinly sliced

1 leek, trimmed and thinly sliced

1 bunch of spring onions (about 6), trimmed
    and sliced

1.2 litres fresh vegetable or chicken stock

sea salt, black pepper

2 ripe tomatoes, cores removed, chopped

70g watercress, coarsely chopped

40g rocket, coarsely chopped

150g feta, crumbled

100g pitted black olives, coarsely chopped

extra virgin olive oil, to serve

Melt the butter in a large saucepan over a medium heat. Add the celery, leek and spring onions and fry gently for about 2 minutes until glossy and just starting to relax. Pour in the stock, season and bring to the boil, then simmer over a low heat for 15 minutes.

Add the tomatoes, watercress and rocket, and then turn up the heat slightly and simmer for 2 minutes. Stir in the feta and black olives and remove from the heat. Taste for seasoning and serve in warm bowls, drizzled with extra virgin olive oil.

Cauliflower cheese soup

Cauliflower has always skirted the fringes of popularity, though I'm not quite sure what it should have done to deserve this. I guess some people might be put off by its texture, and this might explain why we so often smother it in silky cheese sauce. Obviously its texture doesn't apply to soup, where its subtle elegant aroma is at the fore, but I'd like to think doubters could be converted here. The cheese sauce is such a great marriage it happily translates to a soup.

Serves 4

800–900g cauliflower florets (about 1 large
    cauliflower)

25g unsalted butter

20g plain flour

600ml chicken or vegetable stock

300ml milk

100ml double cream

sea salt, black pepper

1 bay leaf

100g grated mature Cheddar

1 teaspoon Dijon mustard

1 teaspoon grainy mustard

freshly grated nutmeg, to serve

Bring a large pan of salted water to the boil, add the cauliflower and simmer for 10 minutes or until it is really tender. Drain into a colander.

Meanwhile, melt the butter in a medium non-stick saucepan, stir in the flour and cook for about 1 minute, or until the roux is seething and floury in appearance. Working off the heat, gradually blend in the stock, milk and cream. Season and add the bay leaf. Bring to the boil, stirring all the time, and then simmer over a low heat for 10 minutes. Discard the bay leaf and stir in the Cheddar and the mustards.

Blend the soup base with the cauliflower in batches in a liquidiser, then return it to a clean saucepan. Reheat to serve, tasting for seasoning and dish up with a grinding of fresh nutmeg.

A soup with spring in its step, courtesy of lots of chopped watercress and rocket. The feta and black olives stirred in at the end ensure this is a really lively bowlful, etched with goodness.

Sweet potato and cumin soup with feta yogurt

Sweet potatoes make for a fab soup, in fact I think this is my favourite way of serving them. Like parsnips and carrots, the result is thick and comforting. All three vegetables can be approached along much the same path, so if you have a particular recipe for one that you love it may well translate with success – they marry well with spices and salty cheeses. It's the orange-fleshed potatoes you want here, rather than the cream-coloured ones.

Serves 6

3 tablespoons extra virgin olive oil
1 large onion, peeled and chopped
4 garlic cloves, peeled and finely chopped
1 heaped teaspoon ground cumin
a pinch of dried chilli flakes
1kg orange-fleshed sweet potatoes, peeled and thickly sliced

1.2 litres chicken or vegetable stock
sea salt
75g feta, crumbled
150g Greek yogurt
2 tablespoons finely chopped sun-dried tomatoes (optional), to serve

Heat the oil in a large saucepan over a medium heat. Add the onion and fry for a few minutes until relaxed and glossy, stirring occasionally. Add the garlic, cumin and chilli and fry for a minute longer. Add the sweet potato, and continue to cook for another couple of minutes, stirring frequently. Pour in the stock and season with salt, bring to the boil and simmer over a low heat for 20 minutes, by which time the potato should be meltingly tender. Liquidise the soup in batches. Return it to the saucepan and season with a little more salt if necessary.

Combine the feta and yogurt in a bowl and serve spooned on top of the soup, scattered with a teaspoon of chopped sun-dried tomato if using.

The Dairy

Chilled cucumber and coriander soup

There should be a definite bite of chilli about this soup as a challenge to the cucumber – go for large chillies that provide flavour as well as heat. The salmon or keta roe can be subsituted for crabmeat or shrimp.

Serves 4

To serve
½ cucumber, peeled and finely sliced
1 rounded teaspoon sea salt
1 rounded teaspoon caster sugar
4 heaped teaspoons salmon or keta roe
Soup
1 x 500g tub of natural yogurt
1 x 200g tub of Greek yogurt

½ cucumber, peeled and roughly cut into pieces
1 heaped teaspoon chopped fresh green chilli
1cm knob of fresh root ginger, peeled
  and chopped
2 handfuls of coriander leaves
1 heaped teaspoon sea salt
1 rounded teaspoon caster sugar

Toss the finely sliced cucumber with the salt and sugar in a bowl and set aside for 30 minutes to draw out the juices. Drain the cucumber into a sieve, rinse thoroughly in cold water to get rid of the salt and sugar, and then drain again. Pat dry on kitchen paper or a tea towel and set aside in a bowl.

To make the soup, place all the ingredients in a liquidiser and blend until smooth and creamy. Taste and add more salt or sugar if necessary.

Pour the soup into bowls and float some of the cucumber slices over the surface. Scatter a heaped teaspoon of roe over the cucumber slices, using your fingers to break it up, and serve straight away.

Chilled spinach and yogurt soup

Lovely slippery inky dark leaves that slip down with a thick creamy yogurt spiked with cumin. I'd eat this soup with some warm unleavened bread, and green olives and olive oil, and perhaps a pickle.

Serves 6

6 tablespoons extra virgin olive oil,
  plus extra to serve
500g baby spinach
3 shallots, peeled and finely chopped

4 garlic cloves, peeled and crushed to a paste
1 heaped teaspoon cumin seeds
sea salt, black pepper
1 x 500g tub of natural yogurt

You will need to cook the spinach in about four goes. Heat a tablespoon of oil in a large frying pan over a medium heat, add a quarter of the spinach and fry, stirring, until it wilts. Transfer to a bowl and cook the remainder in the same way, then coarsely chop it on a board.

Heat a couple of tablespoons of oil in a large saucepan over a medium heat and fry the shallots for several minutes until softened and lightly coloured. Stir in the garlic and cumin, and then add the spinach and plenty of seasoning and stir again. Add 500ml water and bring to the boil, then stir in the yogurt. Pour into a bowl and leave to cool completely. You can either eat it at room temperature, or cover and chill for a couple of hours in the fridge. Serve with a drizzle of extra virgin olive oil.

Warming chicken and rice soup

A packet of chicken drumsticks is the starting point here (or drumsticks and thighs if that's how they come). Not only do they provide a basic stock but lovely slippery little shreds of flesh as well.

Cooking with yogurt calls for house rules, or a rule – when it forms the base of a hot soup it needs to be stabilised to prevent it from splitting. Here it is combined with egg yolk and flour before heating through, but even then it is best to avoid boiling it. This is quite a hearty soup, so it's main course stuff.

Serves 6

4 tablespoons extra virgin olive oil
sea salt, black pepper
8 free-range chicken drumsticks or thighs
50g basmati rice
1 medium onion, peeled and finely chopped
5 garlic cloves, peeled and finely chopped

6 tablespoons finely chopped mint
2 medium organic egg yolks
1 heaped teaspoon plain flour
1 x 450g tub of Greek yogurt
paprika (optional), to serve

Heat a couple of tablespoons of olive oil in a large saucepan over a medium heat, season the drumsticks and colour them on all sides. Add 900ml water, bring to the boil and then cover and simmer over a low heat for 30 minutes. Meanwhile, place the rice in a bowl, cover with plenty of cold water and leave to soak for 30 minutes, then drain. Transfer the cooked drumsticks to a bowl, reserving the stock in the pan. Leave the chicken until cool enough to handle, and then remove and dice the flesh.

Heat the remaining olive oil in a medium saucepan over a medium heat and fry the onion for about 5 minutes until lightly coloured, stirring occasionally. Stir in the garlic and half the mint and cook for a moment until fragrant, then add the rice and stir until coated in the oil. Skim off any excess fat from the chicken stock, and then add it to the pan. Bring to the boil, cover and simmer over a low heat for 12–15 minutes until the rice is just tender.

Meanwhile, whisk the egg yolks with the flour in a small bowl. Whisk in about a tablespoon of the Greek yogurt, and then stir the mixture back into the yogurt.

Add the diced chicken to the soup and heat through. Whisk a ladleful of the hot soup into the yogurt to thin it, and then stir this back into the soup. Turn the heat up a little so that the soup is almost boiling – until the odd bubble breaks the surface – and then stir in the rest of the mint and taste for seasoning. Serve in warm bowls, dusted with paprika if you like.

Curried coconut yogurt soup

This soup tastes richer than the ingredients suggest, which is down to the yogurt base. It derives from the Indian restaurant Zaika in West London, who have an enlightened approach to Indian cooking, which can so often be heavy. I particularly love the little crunchy black mustard seeds in all that milky sweetness. As ever, the chicken brochettes on the side are optional, but delicious – you could always double up and have them with a salad to follow.

Serves 4

225g natural yogurt
20g gram flour, sifted
350ml light chicken stock or water
2 tablespoons vegetable oil
2 teaspoons black mustard seeds
2–3cm knob of fresh root ginger, peeled and finely chopped

1 garlic clove, peeled and thinly sliced
1 medium-hot green chilli, seeds removed, sliced
3 whole red chillies
1 x 400ml tin of coconut milk
sea salt
2 tablespoons finely chopped coriander
15g unsalted butter, to serve

In a large bowl, blend the yogurt and gram flour with the chicken stock or water and whisk until smooth. Heat the oil in a medium saucepan, add the mustard seeds and once these fizzle add the ginger, garlic, chopped green chilli and whole red ones. Give everything a stir, and then add the yogurt and gram flour mixture and bring to the boil, stirring. Pour in the coconut milk, season the soup generously with salt and bring back to the boil. Simmer for a couple of minutes. Strain the soup through a sieve into a bowl and return it to the pan.

Gently reheat the soup, stir in the fresh coriander and serve in warm cups or bowls with a knob of butter in the centre, accompanied by the chicken brochettes if you wish (see right).

Chicken brochettes

1 teaspoon chopped red chilli, seeds removed

1 teaspoon cumin seeds

1 teaspoon coriander seeds

1 teaspoon finely chopped coriander

juice of ½ lemon

1 tablespoon vegetable oil

sea salt

2 skinless free-range chicken breasts,
*   cut into 2cm dice*

Heat the chilli, cumin and coriander seeds in a small frying pan until they release their aroma, and then grind the mixture in an electric grinder (a coffee grinder will do). Remove to a bowl and add the fresh coriander, lemon juice, vegetable oil and a little salt. Add the chicken and coat it with the spice mixture, and then leave to marinate while you prepare the soup.

Thread the chicken onto four 20cm metal skewers or soaked bamboo ones. Heat a large frying pan or ridged griddle over a medium-high heat, and cook the chicken on all sides for about 7 minutes in total.

Parsley soup with saffron cream

Serves 4

a pinch of saffron filaments (about 20)

25g unsalted butter

2 medium onions, peeled and chopped

2 large bunches (about 200–250g) flat-leaf
   parsley (stalks and leaves), ends trimmed

2 tablespoons basmati rice

1 litre vegetable stock or water

sea salt, black pepper

2 tablespoons crème fraîche

Infuse the saffron filaments in a teaspoon of boiling water. Melt the butter in a medium saucepan over a medium heat and fry the onions and the parsley stalks for a few minutes until softened.

Add the rice and the vegetable stock or water and bring to the boil. Simmer for about 15 minutes, adding the parsley leaves a few minutes before the end. Liquidise and season to taste, and then ladle into warm bowls. Blend the saffron liquor with the crème fraîche and serve drizzled over.

Spring vegetable soup with yogurt

The vegetables will be at their brightest green when the soup is freshly made, as the acidity in the yogurt will cause them to dull in colour. Use the list as a guide and include whatever vegetables you happen to have, providing they are spring-like and green – asparagus, sugar snaps and broad beans all come to mind.

Serves 4

2 medium organic egg yolks

1 heaped teaspoon plain flour

1 x 450g tub of Greek yogurt

800ml vegetable or chicken stock

sea salt, black pepper

200g broccoli florets, trimmed and
   roughly chopped

100g mangetouts, topped and tailed, and then
   roughly chopped

300g fresh or frozen peas

3 spring onions, trimmed and sliced

1 tablespoon chopped tarragon

4 tablespoons chopped flat-leaf parsley

50g toasted flaked almonds (optional), to serve*

Whisk the egg yolks with the flour in a small bowl, and then whisk in a tablespoon of the Greek yogurt. Stir this mixture back into the tub of yogurt.

Bring the stock to the boil in a medium saucepan and season it. Add the broccoli and cook for 3 minutes, then add the mangetouts, fresh peas and spring onions and cook for a further 3–4 minutes or until the vegetables are tender. If using frozen peas, cook them separately to avoid losing the boiling point.

Whisk a little of the soup liquor into the yogurt mixture, and then stir this back into the soup and heat almost to boiling point – until a bubble or two breaks the surface. Stir in the herbs. Whizz the soup in batches in a food processor so that it still retains a bit of texture – if you prefer it smooth, you could use a liquidiser. Taste for seasoning and serve scattered with toasted almonds if you like.

* To toast almonds, arrange them in a thin layer on a small baking dish and bake for 7–8 minutes at 180°C fan oven/200°C electric oven.

A really simple parsley soup, which demonstrates just how much of this herb you can get away with including without it becoming overpowering. The more you add the cleaner and more refreshing the soup seems to become.

Butternut squash soup with truffle cream

In northern Italy entire restaurants are devoted to truffles, where every single dish is permeated with their scent. Black winter truffles (*Tuber melanosporum*), summer truffles (*Tuber aestivum*) and white ones (*Tuber magnatum*) are used in minute quantities to cast a heady cloak over pasta and risottos, a plate of raw beef or a cheese fondue. Once familiar with their perfume it is easy enough to understand the Italians' passion for them, and also their sky-high price, being as rare as they are. Summer truffles are the most common, and they are the ones we usually encounter here, preserved whole in small jars, but you occasionally see the black winter truffles too – albeit at a price. We can tap into the scent of the white ones courtesy of tiny bottles of pungent truffle-flavoured oil, a few drops of which will leave you with the lingering suggestion of it long after you have finished the last mouthful. Like most ingredients in this league, there is no need for a host of other flavours or complication, the scent is so magnificent it says it all.

The soup relies on a potato masher rather than a blender, so it's on the rustic side, and that suave little spoonful of cream makes all the difference. You may like to serve some crisp fried croutons with the soup (see page 165).

Serves 4

50g unsalted butter
200g rindless unsmoked back bacon, diced
3 leeks, trimmed and sliced
2 x 800g butternut squash, skinned, seeded and
    coarsely diced (about 1kg of flesh once the
    skin and seeds are removed)

150ml white wine
1.2 litres chicken stock
sea salt, black pepper
150ml soured cream
1 teaspoon truffle oil

Melt the butter in a large saucepan over a medium heat, add the bacon and fry for 6–8 minutes until lightly coloured and starting to crisp, stirring occasionally. Add the leeks and sauté for about 5 minutes until soft and glossy, and just starting to colour. Add the butternut squash and cook for 10 minutes over a low heat, again stirring occasionally. Pour in the wine and simmer until syrupy and well-reduced. Now add the chicken stock and season with black pepper and a little salt, bearing in mind the bacon will do some of the work. Bring to the boil and simmer for 20 minutes. Using a potato masher, mash the butternut squash until you have a thick, sloppy purée. Taste to check the seasoning.

Blend the soured cream and truffle oil in a small bowl. Serve the soup in warm bowls with the truffle cream spooned in a swirl and a scattering of croutons on top if you wish (see page 165).

The Fishmonger

For many of us, our first taste of the Mediterranean is inextricably linked to our first taste of 'soupe de poisson,' that rich, thick golden soup that we might otherwise have turned our nose up at were it not for the crisp slivers of baguette, the heady rust-coloured rouille and grated Gruyère that melted into the soup when you floated your crouton. It left us with a sense of taking our first step into an adult world, as did a bowl of moules marinière. I find it heartening how young children will take to working their way through a pile of these black molluscs, relishing the hands-on ritual, justification for getting seriously messy. Even now, I find fish soups have a sense of being special, they're celebratory, regardless of how humble the fish.

White vegetable soup with smoked haddock

Not really a fish soup at all, but another way of looking at things, where just a little fish stretches a long way – a silky smooth cauliflower and turnip soup topped with salty, buttery flakes of smoked haddock. If you want to omit the crème fraîche for a lighter soup, then increase the chicken stock by 100ml.

Serves 6

25g unsalted butter
1 cauliflower, cut into small florets
2 large turnips, peeled and diced
2 medium onions, peeled and chopped
900ml chicken stock
sea salt, white pepper
100g crème fraîche
freshly grated nutmeg

To serve
400g undyed smoked haddock fillet
25g unsalted butter, plus an extra knob
1 bay leaf
a squeeze of lemon juice
1 tablespoon snipped chives

Melt the butter in a large saucepan over a low heat and fry the cauliflower, turnip and onion for about 20 minutes, stirring occasionally, until glossy but without allowing them to colour. Add the stock and some seasoning, bring to the boil, and then cover and cook over a low heat for 15 minutes. Purée the soup in batches in a liquidiser with the crème fraîche, and season with nutmeg, and more salt and pepper if necessary.

Cut the smoked haddock to fit the base of a medium saucepan. Add a few millimetres of water, dot with 25g butter and tuck in the bay leaf. Bring to the boil, cover and cook over a low heat for 5 minutes. Transfer the fish to a plate and coarsely flake, discarding the skin. The soup and fish can be prepared to this point a few hours in advance, in which case cover and set aside in a cool place.

When you are ready to serve, reheat the soup. Melt a knob of butter in a small saucepan, add the flaked haddock and gently reheat. Season with a squeeze of lemon juice and stir in the chives. Ladle the soup into bowls and serve with the haddock in the centre.

Crab and fennel soup

For ease I usually buy my crab ready-cooked or, picked over and at the ready in a tub or shell.

Serves 6

3–4 tablespoons extra virgin olive oil
3 fennel bulbs (about 900g), trimmed and chopped
3 sticks of celery heart, sliced
3 slim carrots, trimmed, peeled and sliced
150ml white wine

1 litre fish stock
zest of 1 lemon, plus a couple of squeezes of juice
sea salt
250g white crabmeat
cayenne pepper
150ml whipping cream, whipped

Heat 3 tablespoons of oil in a large saucepan over a medium heat, add half the vegetables and fry for 8–10 minutes until soft and translucent, stirring occasionally. Transfer these to a bowl and cook the remainder in the same way, adding a little more oil to the pan if necessary. Return all the vegetables to the pan. Add the wine and simmer until well reduced. Add the stock, lemon zest and some salt, bring to the boil, and then cover and simmer for 20 minutes.

Liquidise the soup in batches in a blender, pass it through a sieve, and then return it to the saucepan. Place the crabmeat in a bowl, pour over some of the hot soup and blend with a spoon, then stir this back into the rest of the soup. Season to taste with lemon juice, salt and cayenne pepper, and reheat gently without boiling. To serve, place a spoonful of cream in the bottom of six bowls and ladle the hot soup over.

Cream of carrot soup with grilled scallops

Like the white vegetable *velouté* on page 72, where the fish is a frill, here a few scallops provide a royal touch for a humble carrot soup – although it is no lesser with a scattering of chopped parsley or chives.

Serves 6

1 litre chicken stock
900g large carrots, trimmed, peeled and sliced
300g crème fraîche
sea salt, black pepper
½ teaspoon caster sugar

To serve
6 medium scallops (about 200g)
groundnut or vegetable oil
a squeeze of lemon juice

Bring the stock to the boil in a large saucepan. Add the carrots, bring back to the boil, and then cover and simmer over a low heat for 15 minutes. Purée the soup in batches in a liquidiser, along with the crème fraîche, a generous addition of salt, a grinding of pepper and the sugar.

Gently reheat the soup to serve. Remove the corals from the scallops, if present, pulling off the girdle that surrounds them and with it the white gristle. Cut this off and discard, reserving the corals and white scallop meat. Slice each scallop into two or three discs. Heat a large, non-stick or cast-iron frying pan over a high heat. Brush the scallops and corals with vegetable oil, seasoning just one side, and grill for 30 seconds on each side. It's easiest to do this in two batches. Squeeze over a little lemon juice. Ladle the soup into bowls and serve with the scallops in the centre.

Pea soup with squid

Richard Olney's recipe for squid stuffed with peas in *Ten Vineyard Lunches* (to be snapped up should you ever come across it in a secondhand bookshop) has for me been a defining moment – I have never wanted to eat this cephalopod any other way since first cooking the dish, although this soup is rather simpler. For anyone averse to the slightly slippery textures that characterise particular foods, the solution is to marry them with their opposite, and this combination of squid with peas is a match made in heaven. Other duos that work well together include shellfish with lentils or coarsely crushed potatoes, and oysters with sourdough bread and unsalted butter. Here the sweet mealy texture of the peas is just right with the squid, and balances out that slippery tendency that in the wrong company can be off-putting.

Serves 4

300g squid
750ml fish stock
3 tablespoons extra virgin olive oil
1 large onion, peeled and chopped
150ml dry vermouth
600g fresh shelled peas

1 teaspoon caster sugar
sea salt, black pepper
10 good-sized basil leaves
225g raw peeled king prawns
a squeeze of lemon juice
2 tablespoons coarsely chopped flat-leaf parsley

Your squid may already be prepared, if not tug to separate the tentacles from the body and discard them. Slip the outer purple film off the pouches, pull out the pen inside and wash out any jelly-like substances from within. Slice off and discard the wings, and cut the pouches into thin rings.

Bring the fish stock to the boil in a small saucepan. Heat 2 tablespoons olive oil in a large saucepan over a medium heat, add the onion and fry for 5–6 minutes until relaxed and just starting to colour, stirring occasionally. Add the dry vermouth and cook until it is syrupy. Add the peas and stir, then add the boiling stock, the sugar and some seasoning. Bring back to the boil and simmer for 5–6 minutes or until the peas are tender.

Pour the soup into a food processor, add the basil leaves and blend to a coarse purée – the soup should still retain some texture. Adjust the seasoning, it may well need more salt, and then return it to the saucepan and reheat gently.

At the same time, heat a tablespoon of olive oil in a large frying pan over a high heat. Add the prawns and sauté for 1 minute, and then add the squid rings and cook for 1 minute more. Season, squeeze over a little lemon juice and toss in the parsley. Serve the soup in warm bowls with the squid and prawns spooned in the centre.

Smoked haddock and potato chowder

One of those classic combinations that is just as successful in Omelette Arnold Bennett as it is in chowder – in fact, a poached egg would sit nicely in a bowlful if you want to go to town here. And without requiring fish stock, this is a great stew to have up your sleeve. The technique is to cook the bacon and leeks in one pan, and the haddock, milk and cream in another and then combine them at the very end. This ensures perfect results without splitting the milk, which can be a risk when everything is cooked together.

Serves 4

40g unsalted butter
7 rashers rindless smoked back bacon,
    cut into 1cm strips
3 leeks, trimmed and sliced
400ml full-cream milk
200ml whipping cream
450g maincrop potatoes,
    peeled and cut into 1cm dice

1 bay leaf
450g undyed smoked haddock fillet,
    skinned and cut into 2cm pieces
black pepper
coarsely chopped flat-leaf parsley, to serve

Melt the butter in a large saucepan over a medium heat, add the bacon and fry for 7–9 minutes, stirring occasionally to separate the pieces, until it is lightly coloured. Add the leeks and continue to fry for about 7 minutes until softened and just starting to colour.

Meanwhile, bring the milk and cream to the boil in another large pan with the potatoes and bay leaf, and simmer over a low heat for about 8 minutes. Add the haddock and poach for 5 minutes until the potatoes are tender and the haddock flakes. Combine the contents of the two saucepans and season with black pepper. Serve in warm soup bowls, scattered with parsley.

Variation ## Seabass and mussel chowder

Traditional New England chowder contains crackers, and it may be that you have access to the authentic item, but water biscuits do a fine job crumbled over at the end. And so you could just as well use clams as mussels, although the latter tend to be much easier to come by – not least because of the success in farming them in northern Europe – and they always promise lots of saline juices, which stand in as a stock in a soup.

Place *500g cleaned mussels* (see page 78) in a large saucepan, and then cover and cook over a high heat for about 4 minutes until they open. Leave the pan half covered with the lid until the mussels are cool enough to handle, and then shell them, reserving the liquor – you should have a little under 100ml.

Include the mussel liquor with the milk and cream, and replace the haddock with sea bass, skinned and cut into 3–4cm pieces. Stir the shelled mussels into the cream base to heat through at the end. Serve scattered with *coarsely crumbled water biscuits* as well as parsley.

Garlic butter mussel pot

One of my favourite starters in small seafood restaurants is a platter of mussels sizzling in a pool of garlicky butter. This recipe couldn't be simpler – you dot the cooked mussels with garlic butter, clamp on a lid and leave it to melt.

Serves 6

70g unsalted butter

3 garlic cloves, peeled and crushed to a paste

juice of ½ lemon

a shake of Tabasco

5 tablespoons finely chopped flat-leaf parsley

3kg cleaned mussels (see below)

3 shallots, peeled and finely chopped

150ml dry white wine

a baguette and unsalted butter, to serve

To make the garlic butter, place the butter, garlic, lemon juice and Tabasco in the bowl of a food processor and whizz until creamy and amalgamated. Add the chopped parsley and give another quick whizz to mix it in. Do not worry if a little of the lemon juice seeps out, most of it will have been incorporated. Transfer the butter to a bowl.

Place the mussels with the shallots and wine in a large casserole, and cover with a tight-fitting lid. Heat the pan over a high heat for about 5 minutes, stirring halfway through, by which time the mussels should have just steamed open. Dot the garlic butter over the mussels, put on the lid and leave for a few minutes, then give them a stir. Accompany with bread and butter.

Variation

More stew than soup...

Strain the mussel juices into a large bowl, reserving the cooked mussels in the pan. Pour the juices into a clean pan, discarding the last little gritty bit of liquid, and boil over a high heat to reduce by half. Meanwhile, dot the mussels with garlic butter, cover with a lid and leave to melt. Pour the reduced juices back over the mussels to serve.

* Give the mussels a good wash in a sink of cold water, discarding any that are broken or that do not close when tapped. Pull off any beards and scrape off any barnacles. If they are very dirty, give them a second rinse.

Provençal red mullet soup

With many fish there are other types that can stand in, but red mullet stands on its own, with its meaty texture and suspicion of oiliness that is in no way pervasive – much as I love mackerel and salmon, they leave you in no doubt that you're getting your full complement of Omega 3. Mullet also has a uniquely rich flavour and soft buttery skin. The main downside are the row of bones running down the centre of each fillet, no problem for restaurants that are at the ready with a pair of tweezers, but here where only small pieces are called for the solution is to cut either side and remove them as a long thin strip. A generous dollop of rich buttercup yellow mayonnaise, and we're somewhere south of Lyon.

Serves 6

3–4 tablespoons extra virgin olive oil,
*   plus extra to serve*
2 large onions, peeled, halved and sliced
2 fennel bulbs, trimmed and chopped
6 garlic cloves, peeled and smashed
1kg ripe plum tomatoes, quartered
a knife tip of dried chilli flakes
2 strips of orange zest, removed with a
*   potato peeler*
150ml white vermouth
1 litre fish stock
sea salt, black pepper
150g baby spinach leaves

600–700g red mullet fillets, cut into 3–4cm pieces
6 thick slices of day-old, coarse-textured white
*   bread, e.g. ciabatta*
60g pitted oily black olives, halved
Saffron mayonnaise
1 medium organic egg yolk
1 teaspoon Dijon mustard
sea salt
300ml groundnut oil
a pinch of saffron filaments (about 20), ground
*   and infused with 1 teaspoon boiling water*
*   for 10 minutes*
a squeeze of lemon juice

First prepare the soup base. As you're going to be straining this, the veg don't have to be perfectly diced. Heat the olive oil in a large saucepan over a medium-high heat, add the onion, fennel and garlic and fry, stirring occasionally, for 8–10 minutes until softened and starting to colour. Add the tomatoes, chilli, orange zest, vermouth, fish stock and a generous dose of salt. Bring to the boil, and then cover and cook over a low heat for 45 minutes. Pass through a sieve into a large bowl, pressing out as much of the juice from the vegetables as possible. Taste for seasoning. The soup can be made up to this point a day in advance, in which case cover and leave to cool, and then chill in the fridge.

To make the saffron mayonnaise, whisk the egg yolk, Dijon mustard and a little salt together in a medium bowl. Very gradually whisk in the groundnut oil, to begin with just a few drops at a time, and then once the mayonnaise has started to emulsify in a more generous stream. Stir in the saffron liquid halfway through, when the mayonnaise seems too thick to whisk, and then continue whisking in the rest of the oil. Season with a squeeze of lemon juice. Store, covered, in the fridge and bring back to room temperature before eating.

Shortly before serving, bring the soup to the boil in a large saucepan or casserole. Stir in the spinach and cook for about a minute. Season the fish with salt and pepper and add to the soup. Bring back to the boil over a medium-high heat, and then simmer for 1 minute. Toast the bread, place one piece in the base of six warm, shallow soup bowls and drizzle with olive oil. Ladle over the soup, and serve with a dollop of saffron mayonnaise and a few olives scattered over.

The Fishmonger

Mussel soup with tomato and chilli

This soup is one of a favourite trio of mussel stews – the hint of chilli with the tomato and mussel juices is especially satisfying, and for those of us in northern climes makes for a great warm weather soup to be eaten on a terrace on a summer's evening.

Serves 4

1.5kg cleaned mussels (see page 78)
150ml white wine
3 garlic cloves, peeled
3 tablespoons extra virgin olive oil, plus extra to serve
4 tablespoons chopped flat-leaf parsley
1 x 400g tin of chopped tomatoes
1 small dried red chilli, finely chopped
4 slices of baguette, 1cm thick

Place the mussels in a large saucepan with the wine. Cover with a lid and cook over a high heat for 5 minutes, by which time they should have opened. Remove them to a bowl, and pour the cooking liquor into a separate jug, discarding the gritty bit at the bottom. Depending on how energetic you're feeling, you may like to shell half the mussels.

Finely chop two of the garlic cloves. Heat the olive oil in a large saucepan over a medium heat, add the chopped garlic and half the parsley and sizzle momentarily until the garlic just begins to colour, then add the tomatoes and chilli. Turn the heat down and cook very gently for about 15 minutes, stirring occasionally, until the oil rises to the surface and separates out from the tomatoes. The soup can be prepared to this point in advance.

To serve, add the mussel juices to the tomato base and heat together, then add the mussels to the pan. Cover and reheat for a couple of minutes, stirring once. Toast the slices of bread, and then give each one a quick rub with the reserved garlic clove. Place the garlicky croutons in the base of four soup bowls, splash over a little olive oil, and then ladle the soup on top. Scatter over the remaining parsley and drizzle with another splash of olive oil.

Curried smoked haddock and potato stew

This comes close to a chowder but, without any bacon, curry spices jostle with the haddock instead. You could also look beyond India to a Middle Eastern spice blend, providing it isn't too hot. Alternatively, stir in some chopped watercress or flat-leaf parsley at the end, or simply relish its rich creaminess with a warm crusty roll.

Serves 6

600ml full-cream milk
300ml whipping cream
450g maincrop potatoes, peeled and cut into 1cm dice
1 bay leaf
600g undyed smoked haddock fillet, skinned and cut into 3–4cm pieces

50g unsalted butter
3 leeks, trimmed and sliced
1 celery heart, trimmed and thinly sliced
3 slim carrots, trimmed, peeled and thinly sliced
2 teaspoons mild curry powder
sea salt, black pepper
a squeeze of lemon juice

Bring the milk and cream to the boil in a large pan with the potatoes and bay leaf, and simmer over a low heat for about 8 minutes. Add the haddock and poach for a further 5–6 minutes or until the potatoes are tender and the haddock flakes.

At the same time, melt the butter in a large saucepan over a medium heat, add the leeks, celery and carrot and fry for about 7 minutes until soft and just starting to colour, then stir in the curry powder. Combine the contents of the two saucepans and season with salt and pepper and a generous squeeze of lemon juice. Serve in warm soup bowls.

Moules marinière

Moules marinière is one of the greatest fish stews/soups, awesome in its simplicity. The small seaside cafés along the Cotentin Peninsula in Normandy use the small, orange *moules de bouchot* farmed in the tidal waters along the coast on wooden stakes. This particular recipe stems from a favourite and very eccentric little café perched on top of the dunes at Blainville-sur-Mer, called La Cale, meaning 'the slipway'.

Serves 2

3 tablespoons groundnut or vegetable oil
2 tablespoons very finely chopped onion
2 tablespoons very finely chopped shallot
1 garlic clove, peeled and finely chopped
100ml white wine

1.7kg cleaned mussels (see page 78)
70g crème fraîche or unpasteurised cream
a handful of coarsely chopped flat-leaf parsley
sourdough bread and unsalted butter, to serve

Heat the oil in a large saucepan over a high heat, add the onion, shallot and garlic and fry for about a minute until softened. Pour in the wine and simmer to reduce by half. Add the mussels, clamp on the lid and cook for 5–6 minutes until opened. Stir in the crème fraîche and parsley and serve with sourdough bread and butter.

A chowder pie

Chowders transport us to some silvered jetty in Maine fringed with pastel clapboard houses, where we can dangle our legs in the cool blue water, or so we wish. The word itself is supposed to derive from the French *chaudière* and thought to have been introduced to Newfoundland by Breton fishermen, possibly inspired by their own tradition of *cotriade* that includes potatoes.

We can't always recreate the exact dishes, especially when it comes to fish stew, a chowder, however, is easier than most. Traditionally it contains salt pork fatback (which for many will most closely translate to lardons), fish or shellfish of many descriptions, often thickened either with flour or potatoes, some milk and ship's crackers. Either way chowder is generous in spirit, and here the essential milkiness is added as a spoonful of cream at the very end.

Serves 4

30g unsalted butter
6 rashers of rindless smoked back bacon, cut into thin strips
100g baby leeks or spring onions, trimmed and thickly sliced
100g baby carrots, trimmed, peeled and thickly sliced on the diagonal
100g purple-sprouting broccoli (florets and tender stems), thickly sliced
100g sugar snaps, ends trimmed and halved
500ml chicken stock
200g undyed smoked haddock fillet, skinned and cut into 1cm dice
150g raw peeled prawns
4 tablespoons coarsely chopped flat-leaf parsley
sea salt, black pepper
1 x 375g packet of ready-rolled puff pastry
1 organic egg yolk blended with 1 tablespoon milk
crème fraîche, to serve

Heat the oven to 190°C fan oven/210°C electric oven. Melt the butter in a large saucepan over a medium heat, add the bacon and fry for 7–9 minutes, stirring occasionally to separate the pieces, until it is lightly coloured. Add the vegetables and continue to fry for another couple of minutes, then remove the pan from the heat.

Add the chicken stock, smoked haddock, prawns, parsley and a little seasoning and stir gently to combine. Divide the soup between four 350–400ml ovenproof bowls or small pie dishes.

Roll the pastry a little thinner than it is on a lightly floured worksurface, and cut out four shapes 1cm bigger than the top of each bowl or pie dish. Brush the rim of each pastry shape with egg wash and place it painted-side down on top of each dish, pressing down carefully around the sides. Cut a couple of small slits in the pastry at opposite sides of each bowl, just inside the rim, and brush with egg wash. Place the bowls inside a roasting dish and bake for 20 minutes. Serve the crème fraîche separately, leaving each diner to cut into the pastry and dollop a spoonful into the soup.

Bourride

I used to make this with monkfish, before it was known to be endangered, but these days I find red snapper is a good choice. I tend to leave the skin on, which is not unpleasant to eat, as it helps hold the morsels together. Any other firm-fleshed, white fish will be good – seabass or bream, and turbot, all of which are farmed, also brill or John Dory – and shellfish too are a welcome addition.

Serves 4

Aioli
2 medium organic egg yolks
6 garlic cloves, peeled and crushed to a paste
sea salt
75ml extra virgin olive oil
75ml groundnut oil
1 teaspoon lemon juice
Croutons
extra virgin olive oil, for shallow frying
12 slices of baguette, 1cm thick
1 garlic clove, peeled
Soup
450ml fish stock
150ml white wine

2 shallots, peeled and finely chopped
1 leek, trimmed and sliced
1 fennel bulb, outer layer and shoots discarded, diced
1 strip of orange zest, removed with a potato peeler
a bouquet garni of a bay leaf and a few thyme and parsley sprigs, tied with string
sea salt, black pepper
600g red snapper fillets, cut into 2–3cm pieces
a pinch of saffron filaments (about 20), ground and infused with 1 tablespoon boiling water
coarsely chopped flat-leaf parsley, to serve

To make the aioli, whisk the eggs yolks, crushed garlic and a pinch of salt together in a large bowl. Gradually whisk in the oils, a few drops at a time to begin with until the mayonnaise takes, and then in a continuous stream. Stir in the lemon juice at the end.

To make the croutons, heat a few millimetres of oil in a large frying pan over a medium heat until it is hot enough to surround a slice of bread with bubbles. Fry the slices of baguette until lightly golden with the consistency of fried bread – crisp at the edges but soft in the middle. Swipe each one with the garlic clove.

Place the stock, wine, vegetables, orange zest, bouquet garni and seasoning in a large saucepan and bring to the boil. Cover and simmer for 10 minutes. Season the fish with salt and add to the pan, bring back to a simmer and cook, covered, for about 3 minutes until the fish is firm. Using a slotted spoon, remove the fish and vegetables to a warm serving dish or bowls, discarding the herbs and peel. Add the saffron infusion to the pan. Pour the broth onto the aioli, whisking to blend. Return to the pan and gently heat until slightly thickened, without boiling. Strain the broth over the fish and vegetables, sprinkle with chopped parsley and accompany with the croutons.

This is second to bouillabaisse in the hall of fame of Provençal fish soups or stews, although it travels more readily, the key to its character being the aioli used to thicken the liquor. And it is truly luxurious, a heady limpid ivory broth with prize morsels of fish.

Normandy fish soup

This is the classic fish soup that is served in nearly all of Normandy's seaside restaurants. This recipe is based on Jean-Christophe Chavaillard's *soupe de poisson* served at his restaurant Le Cap a L'Ouest overlooking the bay of Mont Saint Michel – a rich aromatic golden soup, dished up with croutons, *rouille* and grated Gruyère, it makes for a sustaining repast. Such soup is often sold in large jars and exported, but these convenience soups have little of the character of the real thing. But the difficulty in making it lies with the selection of fish normally used, a large pile of turbot, sole bones, conger eel and small swimming crabs known as *etrilles*. And then of course you need a mixer with industrial strength to break down the shells and bones when it is puréed. So this is a home-friendly take on it, shell-on shrimps can replace the brown crab meat, and you can vary the other fish if red gurnard and squid are not available. This soup is inevitably quite a lot of work, but it can be made in advance and also freezes well.

Serves 6–8

6 tablespoons extra virgin olive oil
4 shallots, peeled and coarsely chopped
3 sticks of celery, sliced
1 fennel bulb, trimmed and chopped
1 leek, trimmed, halved lengthways and sliced
2 carrots, trimmed, peeled and sliced
700g very ripe tomatoes, quartered
4 garlic cloves, peeled and sliced
50g parsley (stalks and leaves), coarsely chopped
1 x 750ml bottle of white wine
400g red gurnard fillets, cut into 2–3cm pieces
400g brown crabmeat

600g squid (cleaned weight), or whiting fillets, cut into 2–3cm pieces
1.5 litres fish stock
100g tomato purée, plus 1 tablespoon
1 small dried red chilli, crumbled
½ teaspoon mild curry powder
paprika
sea salt, black pepper
1 teaspoon unsalted butter blended with 1 teaspoon plain flour
crème fraîche, thin slices of toasted baguette, finely grated Gruyère and rouille *(see page 92), to serve*

Heat the olive oil in a large saucepan over a medium heat and fry the shallots, celery, fennel, leek and carrot for 10–15 minutes until lightly golden, stirring occasionally. Add the tomatoes, garlic and parsley and continue to cook for 10–12 minutes until really mushy, stirring occasionally. Add the white wine, bring to the boil and cook over a lively heat to reduce by about three-quarters.

Add the fish, fish stock, 100g tomato purée, the chilli, curry powder, a little paprika and some seasoning. Bring to the boil and simmer over a low heat for 20 minutes, skimming the suface foam when necessary. Whizz the soup in batches in a liquidiser and press through a sieve. Return the soup to the pan, stir in the remaining spoon of tomato purée to give the soup some colour. Add the butter and flour paste in small pieces and simmer until melted.

Serve in warm bowls with a spoon of crème fraîche if wished, accompanied by the croutons, Gruyère and *rouille* – first spread the crouton with *rouille*, pile it with Gruyère and float in the soup.

A simple bouillabaisse

When we think of fish soup, more often than not we think of *bouillabaise*, which of all the regional fish soups along the Mediterranean is the one that is most celebrated. Few of us, however, will ever have actually eaten an authentic Marseillaise *bouillabaise*, something I regard as a positive rather than a negative; it is a dish that perfectly illustrates regionality or the special characteristics acquired when it is produced within a specified area.

You can only experience a true *bouillabaise* in the environs of Marseille, and even then given the depletion of local fish stocks, it will probably continue to evolve further over the years from its starting point centuries ago as a poor fisherman's make-do supper, using the least valuable of the day's catch boiled up in a pan of seawater. Whatever the subsequent inclusion of tomatoes, saffron and other aromatics, it traditionally contains three fish specific to the region.

The most famed of these, and the most elusive is *rascasse* or scorpion fish, a bony specimen that I have never even found in Normandy, a haven for fish cooks and hardly a million miles away. Conger eel and *grondin* perhaps. The other defining features of a *bouillabaise* are the serving of the broth separately from the fish, with croutons and *rouille*, a spicy garlic fest of a sauce, and particular aromatics that we associate with Provence – fennel, saffron, thyme, bay and often orange is used to scent the soup.

Any fish soup should be approached on the basis of what is available locally and sustainably sourced, and in Britain (or elsewhere in the world) that calls for a broad interpretation of the fish included. I am also inclined to dish up a single hearty bowl of soup rather than to separate out the fish from the broth, not least because to be authentic the fish would be cooked unfilleted and overcooks by the time it has flavoured the broth. Filleted fish, which take no more than minutes to cook through is surely preferable. So the starting point is to cheat with a good ready-made fish stock and from there you want the interest provided by several different types of fish, but pretty much any selection of filleted fish will be fine. You need 1–1.2kg in total which is a fair quantity, so I'd look to make some farmed fish part of the line up.

Serves 6

4 tablespoons extra virgin olive oil

2 large onions, peeled, halved and sliced

2 fennel bulbs, trimmed and chopped

6 garlic cloves, peeled and smashed

1kg ripe plum tomatoes, quartered

a knife tip of dried chilli flakes

a good pinch of saffron filaments (about 20)

a few parsley stalks

a few sprigs of thyme

1 strip of orange zest, removed with a potato peeler

100ml white wine

1 litre fish stock

sea salt, black pepper

500g small waxy potatoes, scrubbed or peeled as necessary

200g scallops

500g seabream fillets, skinned and central bones cut out, cut into 3–4 cm pieces

500g seabass fillets, skinned and central bones cut out, cut into 3–4 cm pieces

thin slices toasted baguette, to serve

continued on the next page

Heat the olive oil in a large saucepan over a medium-high heat, add the onion, fennel and garlic and fry, stirring occasionally, for 8–10 minutes until softened and starting to colour. Add the tomatoes, chilli, saffron, parsley, thyme, orange zest, wine, fish stock and a generous dose of salt. Bring to the boil, cover and cook over a low heat for 45 minutes, then pass through a sieve, pressing out as much of the juice from the vegetables as possible. Taste for seasoning. The soup can be made up to this point a day in advance.

Up to an hour or two before serving, bring a large pan of salted water to the boil and cook the potatoes for 15–20 minutes until tender, then drain them into a colander. To prepare the scallops, pull the corals away from the scallop meats and cut off and discard the girdle and white gristle. Halve the scallop meats into two discs and reserve with the corals, and the other fish pieces. Cover and chill until required.

Shortly before serving, bring the soup to the boil in a large cast-iron casserole, season the fish with salt and pepper and add to the soup with the potatoes. Bring back to the boil over a medium high heat and simmer for 2 minutes. Ladle the soup into warm bowls and accompany with croutons and the *rouille*.

On the side ## Rouille

Despite its North African derivation, harissa is exactly what *rouille* or 'rust' calls for. Another shortcut here is to buy red peppers in a jar rather than roasting your own.

15g day-old white bread (weight without crusts)
½ red pepper, roasted, skinned and deseeded
2 garlic cloves, peeled
1 teaspoon harissa
1 large egg yolk
125ml extra virgin olive oil

125ml groundnut oil
a pinch of saffron filaments (about 20),
   ground and infused with 1 tablespoon
   boiling water
lemon juice
sea salt

Place the bread, red pepper, garlic and harissa in a food processor and reduce to a paste. Add the egg yolk, then trickle in the oils in a thin stream as though making a mayonnaise. Stir in the saffron liquid and season with lemon juice and salt.

Romesco de peix

This Catalan fish stew owes its deliciously sweet and aromatic nature to the *romesco* used to thicken it. A red pepper sauce, made with ground nuts, here it thickens the fish broth in the same way that an aioli is used in France, but the result is gutsier and altogether more rustic. I used to make this using monkfish instead of the bream suggested, which is more traditional, but conscience and a little rationale suggest that the stew will be just as good using a less threatened species. Should you have access to any small clams, these can be included as well as, or instead of, the mussels.

Serves 4

12 whole skinned almonds

1 slice of white bread

4 tablespoons extra virgin olive oil,
    plus extra for brushing

4 ripe tomatoes, halved

3 garlic cloves, peeled

1 teaspoon sweet paprika

a pinch of saffron filaments (about 20)

1 teaspoon sherry vinegar

125ml white wine

1 large onion, peeled and chopped

2 red peppers, core, seeds and membranes
    removed, thinly sliced

300ml fish stock

500g sea bream fillets, skinned and cut into
    3–4cm pieces

sea salt, black pepper

500g cleaned mussels (see page 78)

Heat the oven to 180°C fan oven/200°C electric oven, lay the almonds out in a small tray and toast for 10 minutes. Meanwhile, heat a ridged griddle over a medium heat for about 5 minutes. Brush the bread on both sides with olive oil and toast on the griddle until golden. Remove and set aside. Now brush the tomatoes with oil and grill them too, cut-side down first, and then the skin for several minutes until striped with gold and softened. Remove from the pan, set aside on a plate and peel off the skins once cool enough.

Break up the toasted bread, place it in the bowl of a food processor and whizz to crumbs. Add the almonds and pulverise, then remove to a bowl and set aside. To make the *romesco* sauce, place the garlic, tomatoes, paprika, saffron, vinegar and wine in the food processor and blitz to a smooth sauce.

Heat the olive oil in a large saucepan over a medium heat, add the onion and sauté for 5 minutes until relaxed. Add the peppers and sauté for a further 10 minutes until the onions are golden and the peppers have softened. Add the *romesco* sauce and the fish stock and bring to the boil. Simmer over a low heat for 20 minutes, stirring occasionally.

To serve, stir the almond breadcrumbs into the simmering soup. Season the sea bream with salt and pepper and add to the pan with the mussels. Bring to the boil, and then cover and cook over a high heat for 5 minutes. Taste for seasoning and ladle into warmed soup bowls.

More Oriental than Mediterranean. Just as you might eat a small
bowl of rice and vegetables with miso soup, here a little aside of egg-fried
rice is the sideshow to a light saffron broth and grilled salmon.

Salmon and saffron broth

Serves 4

a pinch of saffron filaments (about 20)

2 tablespoons groundnut oil, plus extra
   for brushing

1 shallot, peeled and finely chopped

150ml dry white vermouth

600ml fish stock

sea salt, black pepper

400g salmon fillet, skin on

200g baby spinach

lemon or lime quarters, to serve

Grind the saffron in a pestle and mortar and infuse for 30 minutes in a tablespoon of boiling water.

Heat a tablespoon of oil in a medium saucepan over a medium heat and sauté the shallot for about a minute until it softens. Add the vermouth and reduce by half. Add the fish stock, the saffron liquor and some seasoning, bring to the boil and then remove from the heat.

Meanwhile, heat a ridged griddle over a medium heat for 5 minutes. Cutting through the skin, slice the salmon fillet across into 1cm strips. Brush the strips with oil on both sides, season on one side only and grill each side for 30–60 seconds (if you are using a non-stick griddle you can omit the oil). You will probably need to cook the salmon strips in batches, reserving them on a plate once they are cooked. At the same time, heat a tablespoon of oil in a large frying pan over a high heat, add the baby spinach and sauté until it wilts. To serve, gently reheat the broth. Divide the spinach between four hot soup bowls, deep or shallow, ladle the broth over and arrange a few salmon strips in the centre. Serve with small bowls of egg-fried rice to the side if you wish (see below) and accompany with lemon or lime wedges.

On the side

Egg-fried rice

200g basmati rice

sea salt, black pepper

2 medium organic eggs

1 tablespoon sesame oil

1 tablespoon groundnut oil

4 spring onions, trimmed and finely sliced

light soy sauce (optional), to serve

Rinse the rice in a sieve under the cold tap and place in a small saucepan with 400ml water and a teaspoon of salt. Bring to the boil and simmer over a low heat for 8 minutes, and then remove from the heat, cover with a lid and leave to stand for 20 minutes.

Fluff up the rice using a fork, and whisk the eggs with the sesame oil and some seasoning in a bowl. Heat the groundnut oil in a large frying pan over a medium heat, add the eggs and then straight away add the rice and stir briskly to coat it. Fry for 2–3 minutes, turning it occasionally, and then remove from the heat and stir in the spring onions. Season with a little soy sauce if you wish.

Thai hot and sour soup

A hot and sour Thai soup must be the culinary equivalent of reaching a mountain summit and taking a deep breath of crystal clean air. Its clarity is piercing, all those little spikes of flavour, and yet it's incredibly light compared to other fish stews – you could finish off a large bowl and still feel as though you could run round the block.

Serves 4

600ml chicken stock

1 stalk of lemongrass, trimmed and thickly sliced

1 teaspoon finely chopped fresh root ginger

3 lime leaves

1 small Thai red chilli, finely sliced

500g cleaned mussels (see page 78)

1 tablespoon groundnut oil

2 small heads of pak choi, stems trimmed and leaves separated

12 raw tiger prawns, shelled*

2 tablespoons fish sauce

2 tablespoons lime juice

2 spring onions, trimmed and finely sliced

1 heaped tablespoon chopped coriander

Place the stock, lemongrass, ginger, lime leaves and chilli in a medium saucepan. Bring to the boil, and then cover and simmer over a low heat for 20 minutes.

Place the mussels in a saucepan, cover and steam open over a high heat for 4–5 minutes. As soon as they are cool enough to handle, reserve about a third of them and shell the remainder. Place these together in a bowl and pour over the juices, discarding the last gritty bit.

Heat the oil in a large frying pan over a medium heat, add the pak choi and sauté for a couple of minutes until the leaves turn dark green and wilt.

Strain the broth, return it to the pan and bring back to the boil. Add the pak choi and the prawns, bring back to the boil and simmer for 1 minute. Stir in the fish sauce and lime juice. Add the mussels, along with their liquor, and heat through. Serve in warm soup bowls, scattered with the spring onions and coriander.

* If your tiger prawns arrive shell-on, carefully peel off their shells and add them to the soup base at the beginning, along with the other aromatics.

Portuguese fish stew

A north wind blows through this soup, with cabbage and potato there are strains of bubble and squeak, and were it not for the chorizo (in the absence of Portuguese *chouriço*) and coriander, it could well be British. Its selling points are its gutsy rusticity, its ease of preparation and its affordability – given the sums that so many fish soups can run to. It's great for all those little-known white fish fillets that greet us on the slab in the name of sustainability, which can be a deterrent when they don't come with a reference. Here you are unlikely to go wrong, so it's a good place to try them out. Dish it up with hearty slabs of grilled coarse-textured bread, splashed with olive oil.

Serves 6

3 ripe plum tomatoes
200g Savoy cabbage, outer leaves discarded
2 tablespoons extra virgin olive oil
200g chorizo sausage (cooked or uncooked), skinned, thickly sliced and diced
900g maincrop potatoes, peeled and cut into 1cm dice

150ml white wine
1.5 litres fish stock
sea salt, black pepper
900g mixed white fish fillets, skinned and cut into 2cm pieces
extra virgin olive oil* and coarsely chopped coriander, to serve

Bring a small pan of water to the boil, cut out a central cone from each tomato, plunge them into the boiling water for about 20 seconds, and then into cold water. Skin and coarsely chop them. Slice the cabbage leaves into fine strands, discarding the tough central veins.

Heat the olive oil in a large saucepan over a medium heat, add the chorizo and fry for a few minutes, stirring frequently, until lightly coloured. Pour off the fat (leave this to harden before throwing away), and then add the potatoes. Give them a stir, and then add the wine and cook to reduce by half. Add the chopped tomatoes and fish stock and bring to the boil. Skim off any surface foam, and then simmer over a low heat for 15 minutes. Coarsely mash the potato using a potato masher and season to taste with salt – the chorizo will have done most of the work here.

To serve, add the cabbage, bring back to the boil and simmer for 5 minutes. Season the fish with salt and pepper, add it to the soup and poach for 5 minutes. Serve in warm bowls with some olive oil poured over and a scattering of chopped fresh coriander.

* A good case here for using your finest estate-bottled oil.

The Butcher

Parsimony is written large in the role of the butcher. Soups have long been a way of making meagre rations stretch, and some of the finest traditions are born of paucity, and the idea of making a little go a long way. A few snippets of bacon, a couple of spicy sausages, or chicken wings and drumsticks, will cast their character into a broth with simmering, leaving a lingering sense of goodness. With the addition of lentils and beans, vegetables and herbs, more expensive cuts can also be stretched to double their worth – relegated to playing second fiddle a modest weight of lamb or pork fillet can be turned into a hearty soup-come-stew. And it's not only the dog who benefits from good relations with the butcher, most will be happy to wrap up unwanted bones for their regulars for the purposes of stock.

Harira

Harira is the most famous soup to come out of Morocco. Traditionally served during Ramadan, the ninth month of the Muslim calendar, it breaks the day's fast at sunset. It is easy to imagine just how good and nourishing it must seem, and why the Moroccans hold it so dear, with its gentle spicing, and the comfort of lentils in a lamb broth.

Harira has a habit of seeming more complicated than it need be, inevitable perhaps when there is a long list of ingredients. Here I have pared it down and there's no frying involved – just a couple of hours of gentle simmering. Neck fillet is especially good for this, but otherwise shoulder will do. You could add a handful or two of fine soup noodles a few minutes before the end of cooking.

Serves 6

1.2kg lamb neck fillet, cut into thick medallions
2 medium onions, peeled and chopped
1 head of garlic, cloves peeled
a small bunch of thyme (about 10 sprigs), tied
sea salt
4 ripe tomatoes
300g yellow split peas, rinsed
4 celery sticks, trimmed and finely sliced
¼ teaspoon crushed chilli flakes

1 teaspoon turmeric
1 teaspoon ground ginger
½ teaspoon ground cinnamon
pinch of saffron filaments (about 20)
1 heaped teaspoon plain flour
juice of ½ lemon
3 tablespoons each finely chopped coriander
    and flat-leaf parsley

Place the lamb in a large cast-iron or other heavy casserole with the onion, garlic cloves, thyme, salt and 2 litres of water. Bring to the boil, skim off the foam that rises to the surface, and then cover and cook over a low heat for 30 minutes. Meanwhile, bring a small pan of water to the boil. Cut out a cone from the top of each tomato, plunge into the boiling water for about 20 seconds and then into a bowl of cold water. Skin and coarsely chop.

Remove the lid from the casserole and add the split peas, celery, chilli, spices and tomatoes. Bring back to the boil, stirring, and then cover and simmer for a further hour. Meanwhile, whisk the flour with the lemon juice in a small bowl.

To serve, stir the lemon juice mixture into the soup, bring back to the boil and simmer for another few minutes to cook the flour. Discard the thyme, stir in the chopped herbs and taste for seasoning. Ladle into warm bowls.

Bigos

This Polish hunters' stew would be even wilder at heart made with a jointed rabbit in lieu of chicken, and venison is not unusual – although it would require longer cooking. *Bigos* varies hugely from one family and region to another, especially in the inclusion of meats. Poland's national dish, it is traditionally served on the second day of Christmas – although it is not uncommon for it to be kept going over the course of a week, and added to before the pot empties in the fashion of a medieval perpetual stew, so don't worry about overcooking. This is cause for one of those dark heavy rye breads to mop up the liquor.

Serves 4–6

1 x 450g jar of sauerkraut
¼ white cabbage, core discarded, finely shredded
sea salt, black pepper
1 tablespoon vegetable oil
2 medium onions, peeled, halved and sliced
110g ready-to-eat stoned prunes, halved

1 garlic clove, peeled and smashed
8 free-range chicken thighs
175g Polish kielbasa (or cooking chorizo sausage), skinned and thinly sliced
750ml chicken stock
150ml white wine

Drain the sauerkraut into a colander and rinse it under cold running water. Place in a medium saucepan and cover with water. Bring to the boil, and then drain into the colander. Return it to the pan, cover with clean water and bring to the boil again, this time simmering it over a low heat for 30 minutes. Prepare the white cabbage in exactly the same way, salting the second lot of water and cooking it for 15 minutes.

While the cabbage is cooking, heat the vegetable oil in a large frying pan over a low heat and cook the onions for 20–25 minutes, tossing frequently, until golden and creamy. Once the sauerkraut and cabbage are cooked, drain them in a colander and combine them in a bowl with the fried onions. Add the prunes and garlic clove, season with salt and pepper and combine well.

Heat the oven to 180°C fan oven/200°C electric oven. Heat the frying pan you used to cook the onions, season the chicken thighs and colour them on both sides, draining the fat as necessary. You will probably need to do this in two batches.

Arrange half the cabbage mixture in the base of a large casserole. Place the chicken on top, scatter over the sliced sausage and top with the remaining cabbage. Season the chicken stock and pour it over the cabbage, along with the white wine. Cover with a lid and cook in the oven for 1½ hours, basting and pressing the cabbage down halfway through. Serve in warm, shallow bowls or on plates.

This takes inspiration from an Iranian or Persian lamb koresh, a stew that often contains rhubarb. Most soups benefit from a little acidity, something we often add by way of a glass of wine, a tomato or two or a little lemon juice at the end, and here the rhubarb takes on that role.

Persian rhubarb soup with herbs

Serves 6

5–6 tablespoons extra virgin olive oil
2 large onions, peeled, halved and thinly sliced
700g lamb neck fillet, cut into 2cm dice
leaves and fine stalks from 2 large bunches
    of parsley (about 100g), coarsely chopped,
    plus extra to serve

50g mint leaves, coarsely chopped
1.5 litres chicken stock
sea salt, black pepper
100g risotto rice, e.g. carnaroli
300g forced rhubarb (trimmed weight),
    cut into 1cm lengths

Heat a couple of tablespoons of oil in a large casserole or saucepan over a medium heat, and fry the onion for 10–15 minutes until golden, stirring frequently. Remove to a bowl, add another tablespoon of oil to the pan and colour the meat – you will need to do this in batches. Reserve with the onions once it is done. Add another tablespoon of oil to the pan, put in the herbs and fry until they wilt. Return the lamb and onions to the pan, add the chicken stock and season with salt and pepper. Bring to the boil, and then cover and simmer for 40 minutes. You can prepare the soup to this point in advance.

Add the rice and simmer, covered, for a further 15 minutes. Finally add the rhubarb and cook for 5 minutes. Serve with fresh parsley scattered over.

Lentil, lamb and frisee broth

Frisee cooks up every bit as well as its relation Belgian chicory, even though it is a little less usual, and its lacey fronds provide a delicate note in the company of lentils.

Serves 6

sea salt, black pepper
700g middle neck lamb chops
2 tablespoons vegetable or groundnut oil
2 medium red onions, peeled, quartered
    and thinly sliced
180g French green lentils, rinsed

1 sprig of rosemary, tied into a piece of muslin
300ml white wine
1.2 litres lamb or chicken stock
½ head of frisee (mid and pale green parts),
    cut into roughly 3cm fronds
coarsely chopped flat-leaf parsley, to serve

Heat the oven to 140°C fan oven/160°C electric oven. Heat a large frying pan over a medium-high heat, season the lamb chops and colour them well on both sides – you will need to do this in batches, tipping out any excess fat as you go along. Heat the oil in a large casserole over a medium heat, add the onion and fry for 10–15 minutes until softened and golden, stirring occasionally. Add the lamb chops, lentils, rosemary, wine, stock and some seasoning. Bring to the boil, skim off any foam from the surface, and then cover and cook in the oven for 1½ hours until the meat is meltingly tender.

Discard the rosemary and remove the chops from the soup to a clean plate. Using two forks, flake the meat off the bones and then stir it back into the soup. You can prepare the soup to this point in advance.

To serve, reheat the soup and stir in the frisee. Ladle into warm bowls and scatter each one with parsley.

Pork and cauliflower stew with sherry and paprika

Here the cauliflower is the star ingredient, set off by the chorizo, sherry and chickpeas that lend a little Spanish charm to the dish and bring out the best in it. Romanesco cauliflower, with its beautifully sculpted minarets, might also find a home here in lieu of the standard ivory variety.

Serves 6

6–8 tablespoons extra virgin olive oil
4 medium onions, peeled, halved and sliced
100g cooking chorizo, diced
½ teaspoon paprika
a pinch of saffron filaments (about 20)
sea salt, black pepper
600g pork fillet, trimmed of fat and cut into
   1cm slices

150ml medium sherry
350g small cauliflower florets
350g small broccoli florets
1 x 400g tin of chickpeas, drained and rinsed
juice of ½ lemon
coarsely chopped flat-leaf parsley, to serve

Heat 3 tablespoons of oil in a large cast-iron casserole over a medium-low heat. Add the onions and fry for 15–25 minutes until syrupy and golden, stirring occasionally and adding the chorizo, paprika and saffron about 5 minutes before the end. Transfer everything to a bowl and keep to one side while you brown the pork. Turn up the heat and add another couple of tablespoons of oil to the pan. You will need to brown the pork in two batches to avoid overcrowding the pan. Season the pork and sear on all sides, transferring it to the bowl with the onions as it's ready, and adding more oil to the pan as necessary.

Return the pork to the pan, along with the onion and chorizo mixture. Add the sherry, 400ml water and some seasoning. Bring to the boil, and then cover and cook over a low heat for 1 hour.

Meanwhile, bring a large pan of salted water to the boil and blanch the cauliflower and broccoli florets for 2 minutes. Drain into a colander.

To serve, heat a tablespoon of oil in a large frying pan over a medium-high heat and fry the cauliflower and broccoli until coloured, seasoning well. You will need to do this in batches. Skim any excess fat off the stew, stir in the chickpeas and vegetables and cover and cook for a couple of minutes until just tender. Stir in the lemon juice, taste for seasoning and serve scattered with parsley.

Beetroot bouillon with steak and horseradish sauce

Beetroot and steak have an affinity with each other. The roots dye the broth a rich Renaissance hue, so this is on the dramatic side with its lily-white horseradish cream. Equally, a teaspoon of grainy mustard is also delicious stirred into the crème fraîche if this feisty root is hard to come by.

Serves 4

2 tablespoons groundnut oil, plus extra
for brushing
1 medium red onion, peeled, halved and
thinly sliced
2 small uncooked beetroot, trimmed, peeled
and finely sliced
150ml red wine

600ml beef stock
sea salt, black pepper
1 x 200g sirloin steak, 1–2cm thick
100g crème fraîche
2 teaspoons finely grated fresh horseradish
100g mangetouts, topped and tailed

Heat a tablespoon of oil in a medium saucepan over a medium heat, add the onion and sauté for a few minutes until softened. Add the beetroot and fry gently for a couple of minutes, turning it now and again. Pour in the wine and reduce by half. Add the beef stock and some seasoning, bring to the boil, and then cover and simmer over a low heat for 20 minutes.

About 5 minutes into simmering the soup, heat a ridged griddle over a medium heat for 5 minutes. Also bring a small pan of water to the boil. Brush the steak on both sides with oil and season it. Sear for about 2 minutes on each side to leave it medium-rare, and then transfer to a board and leave to rest for 5 minutes.

Gently blend the crème fraîche and horseradish in a small bowl with a pinch of salt – don't stir too vigorously or the mixture will thicken and curdle. Blanch the mangetouts in the boiling water for 1 minute, and then drain into a sieve. Cut the fat off the steak and slice it across into long strips.

Divide the beetroot soup between four warm, deep bowls. Place a few strips of steak to one side of each bowl and a pile of mangetouts to the other. Dollop a spoonful of the horseradish sauce in the middle and serve straight away.

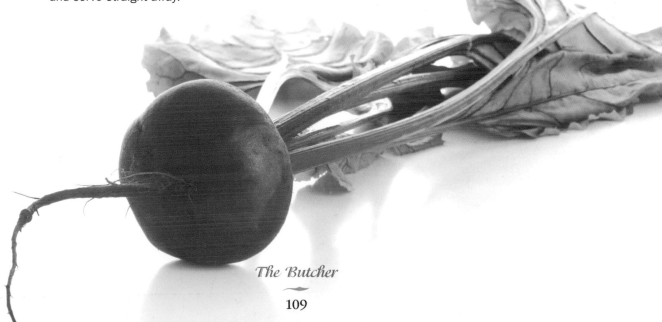

The Butcher

Spinach and beef stew with olives and pickled lemon

An inky green courtesy of the spinach that is its mainstay, while olives and pickled lemons keep you on your toes. The best part is the rich juice, so treat it as you will, my mind wanders to a crisp green lightly dressed salad.

Serves 6

3–4 tablespoons extra virgin olive oil

600g diced stewing beef (chunks roughly 3cm)

sea salt, black pepper

2 medium onions, peeled, halved and thinly sliced

3 garlic cloves, peeled and crushed to a paste

1 teaspoon ground cumin

¼ teaspoon ground allspice

a pinch of dried chilli flakes

600g baby spinach leaves

150g pitted green olives

a squeeze of lemon juice

To serve

3 baby pickled lemons, finely sliced and seeds removed

a couple of handfuls of coriander leaves

You will need to brown the meat in batches. Heat a couple of tablespoons of oil in a large cast-iron casserole over a high heat, add the meat, season and sear to colour it all over. Remove to a clean plate while you brown the rest; keep to one side. Turn the heat down to medium, add the onion and fry for 5–7 minutes until coloured, stirring occasionally. Stir in the garlic and spices, and then add the meat back to the pan. Add 600ml water and some salt and bring to the boil. Cover and cook over a low heat for 2 hours until the meat is tender.

Towards the end of this time, cook the spinach – you will need to do this in 3–4 batches. Heat a tablespoon of oil in a large frying pan over a high heat, add a pile of spinach and fry it until it wilts, stirring. Transfer to a bowl and repeat with the remainder.

Stir the spinach and olives into the stew base and heat through, and then season with a squeeze of lemon juice. Combine the sliced pickled lemon and coriander in a bowl and serve as a little relish on top of the stew.

Chicken mulligatawny

I took this soup on board after my eldest son started to work his way through endless cartons of a supermarket version. Even better than lentil soup, it contains shreds of chicken and that classic trio of ginger, garlic and chilli, with lots of goodies sprinkled over at the end.

Serves 6

1 tablespoon groundnut or vegetable oil
sea salt, black pepper
4 free-range chicken thighs
4 free-range chicken drumsticks
1–2 medium-hot red chillies, deseeded and
*   finely sliced*
2 tablespoons finely chopped fresh root ginger
6 garlic cloves, peeled and finely sliced
6 shallots, peeled, halved and finely sliced
1 teaspoon turmeric

½ teaspoon ground cumin
½ teaspoon ground coriander
350g yellow split peas, rinsed
1.2 litres chicken stock
1 x 400ml tin of coconut milk
3–4 tablespoons lemon juice
To serve
coarsely chopped coriander, finely sliced spring
*   onions, finely sliced red chilli and coarsely*
*   chopped roasted peanuts*

Heat the oil in a large saucepan over a medium-high heat. Season the chicken pieces and colour them on all sides, and then remove them to a bowl. Turn the heat down, add the chilli, ginger, garlic and shallot and fry briefly until softened and aromatic, stirring occasionally. Stir in the spices and the split peas and return the chicken to the pan. Add the stock and season with salt. Bring to the boil, and then cover and simmer for 45 minutes until the split peas are tender and the chicken is coming away from the bone. Give the soup a stir towards the end to make sure the split peas aren't sticking.

Transfer the chicken pieces to a board or plate and shred the flesh, discarding the skin and bones. Return the chicken to the soup, add the coconut milk and bring back to the boil. Season to taste with lemon juice and more salt if necessary. Serve in warmed bowls scattered with the coriander, spring onions, chilli and peanuts.

Lamb and butternut stew with pine nuts

Serves 6

5–6 tablespoons extra virgin olive oil

600g diced leg of lamb (chunks roughly 3cm)

sea salt, black pepper

3 medium onions, peeled, halved and sliced

10 garlic cloves, peeled and thinly sliced

½ teaspoon ground allspice

½ teaspoon ground cinnamon

1 x 400g tin of chopped tomatoes

1 x 900g butternut squash

30g pine nuts

30g coarsely chopped flat-leaf parsley

30g coarsely chopped coriander

juice of ½ lemon

You will need to brown the lamb in batches. Heat a couple of tablespoons of oil in a large cast-iron casserole over a high heat, add half the lamb, season and sear to colour it all over. Transfer this to a bowl while you brown the rest of the meat, adding a little more oil to the pan if necessary. Keeping the meat to one side, turn the heat down to medium and fry the onions for 8–10 minutes until golden, stirring occasionally. Add the garlic towards the end and fry gently for a minute or so. Stir in the spices, and then add the tomatoes. Return the lamb to the pan, pour in 400ml water and season with salt and pepper. Bring to the boil, and then cover and cook over a low heat for 1¼ hours or until the lamb is tender.

Meanwhile, cut the skin off the squash and chop it in half to separate the bulb from the trunk. Quarter the bulb, remove the seeds and slice into wedges; halve the trunk lengthways and cut into slices 1cm thick. When the stew is nearly ready, you can start cooking the squash – you will need to do this in batches. Heat a couple of tablespoons of oil in a large frying pan over a high heat, add half the squash, season and colour it on both sides. Remove to a clean plate while you brown the rest, again removing it at the end. Toast the pine nuts in the same pan, stirring constantly until golden. Reserve on a separate plate.

Once the lamb is cooked then stir the squash into the stew. Cover and cook for about 10 minutes until the squash is tender. To serve, stir in the herbs and lemon juice, taste for seasoning and scatter with the pine nuts.

This spicy Middle Eastern stew is another of those half and half dishes — there is as much butternut squash as there is meat. The result is too soupy to merit ladling over rice, some lovely flatbread would be more in order.

Pot au feu

I love this take on the classic French assembly for its clear broth and the way the vegetables retain their colour and shape. It is a simplified line-up, and a lighter one than the norm. The French would drink the soup and then eat the meat and vegetables separately, either hot with some gherkins and mustard, or cold with a vinaigrette, at which point buttery waxy potatoes or cold ones could come into play. The basil purée is optional, another thought is horseradish sauce* and chopped parsley scattered over.

Serves 4

1 tablespoon groundnut oil

900g top rump, trimmed of fat, cut into
    5cm chunks

200g smoked streaky bacon, rind on, cut into
    rashers 1cm thick and then into 2cm pieces

sea salt, black pepper

4 leeks, trimmed and cut into 2cm chunks

4 medium carrots, trimmed, peeled and sliced
    on the diagonal 2cm thick

1 celery heart, trimmed and cut into 2cm pieces

2 bay leaves

5 sprigs of thyme

Basil purée

1 garlic clove, peeled and chopped

50g basil leaves

6 tablespoons extra virgin olive oil

You will need to brown the meat in batches to avoid overcrowding the pan. Heat the groundnut oil in a large cast-iron casserole over a medium heat, add half the beef and bacon and sear on all sides. Remove to a clean plate while you cook the rest. Return all the seared meat to the pan, add 1.8 litres water, 1½ teaspoons of salt and some black pepper. Slowly bring to a simmer, skimming off the greyish foam as it rises to the surface. Add all the remaining ingredients for the stew, bring back to a simmer, and then cover and cook over a low heat for 2 hours.

To make the basil purée, blend the garlic, basil, olive oil and some seasoning in a food processor and reduce to a smooth purée.

To serve, remove the bay leaf and thyme from the stew and ladle into bowls, placing a spoonful of the basil purée in the centre of each. Remove the bacon rind as you go.

* For the simplest and best horseradish sauce, gently blend 1 x 200g tub of crème fraîche with 2–3 tablespoons finely grated horseradish and season with salt.

Broad bean and chicken stew with pomegranate

This is a topsy-turvy stew. First you poach your chicken, which creates a stock and a few morsels of meat, and then you lightly cook the vegetables in the stock before throwing in lots of herbs at the end.

Serves 6

Chicken base

3–4 tablespoons extra virgin olive oil

sea salt, black pepper

6 pieces of free-range chicken, for example
    thighs and drumsticks

1 onion, peeled and halved

1 bay leaf

1 cinnamon stick, about 7cm in length

Stew

3 medium onions, peeled and chopped

2 celery sticks, trimmed and sliced

4 garlic cloves, peeled and finely chopped

400g leeks (trimmed weight), sliced

½ teaspoon ground ginger

¼ teaspoon allspice

500g cooked baby broad beans*

400g small turnips, peeled and cut into
    thin wedges or diced

several large handfuls of coarsely chopped
    coriander

several large handfuls of coarsely chopped dill

juice of ½–1 lemon

seeds of 1 pomegranate, to serve

Heat a couple of tablespoons of oil in a large cast-iron casserole over a high heat. Season the chicken pieces and add to the pan, colouring them on all sides. Spoon off the excess fat, add 600ml water, the halved onion, bay leaf and cinnamon stick. Don't worry if the chicken isn't completely covered. Bring to the boil, and then cover and cook over a low heat for 1 hour until the chicken is tender. Carefully lift out the chicken pieces and strain the liquor into a large bowl.

Heat 2 tablespoons of oil in the cleaned out casserole over a medium heat. Add the chopped onion and celery and fry for several minutes until softened, stirring occasionally. Put in the garlic and leeks and cook for a couple of minutes. Stir in the ginger and allspice, add the broad beans and turnips, and pour in the chicken poaching liquor. Season with salt and pepper. Bring to the boil, and then cover and simmer for 15 minutes.

Meanwhile, shred the chicken flesh, discarding the skin and bones. To serve, add the chicken to the soup and heat through. Stir in the herbs and lemon juice, taste for seasoning and scatter with the pomegranate seeds.

* I normally use frozen baby broad beans, and cook them according to the instructions on the packet. If using fresh ones, simmer for about 7 minutes until tender.

Chicken and mushroom noodle pot

This is a noodle pot, in the Eastern scheme of things, a very light broth with noodles, chicken and mushrooms. There is nothing worse than an insipid liquor, so this calls for a really good homemade chicken stock, and I tend to reduce it by about a third to enrich its flavour.

Serves 4

2 skinless free-range chicken breasts
1 tablespoon groundnut oil, plus extra
* for brushing*
sea salt, black pepper
600ml good homemade chicken stock
1 tablespoon dry sherry
2 tablespoons light soy sauce
50g fine rice noodles

2 shallots, peeled and finely chopped
150g mixed wild mushrooms, picked over and
* sliced if necessary*
To serve
1 medium-hot red chilli, deseeded, finely sliced
3 spring onions, trimmed and sliced on the
* diagonal*
coarsely chopped coriander

Heat a ridged griddle over a medium heat for 5 minutes, brush the chicken breasts on both sides with oil and season them. Grill for 3–4 minutes on each side until the outside is charred with golden stripes, and the breast feels firm when prodded with your finger. Remove to a chopping board and leave to rest for 5 minutes.

Bring the chicken stock to the boil in a small saucepan, and then remove from the heat and stir in the sherry and soy sauce. Place the noodles in a bowl, cover with boiling water and stir to separate them. Leave to soak for 3 minutes or as directed on the packet. Heat a tablespoon of oil in a large frying pan over a medium heat, add the shallots and sauté for about a minute until they soften. Add the mushrooms and sauté for a few minutes to soften them, seasoning halfway through.

To serve, drain the noodles into a sieve and divide between four warm deep soup bowls. Spoon the mushrooms to the side and ladle over the soup liquor. Slice the chicken breasts and arrange a few slices in the centre of each bowl of soup. Scatter with the chilli, spring onion and coriander.

The Butcher

Poule au pot

Despite the way my Normandy elderly neighbour's eyes mist over as he describes his mother's *poule au pot*, I have yet to have any success cooking this dish with the real bird, which is older than a roasting chicken. The resulting stock may indeed be delicious, and perhaps that is what such birds are best reserved for, but the flesh itself, which is traditionally enjoyed with a simple cream sauce, tends to be dry and unpleasantly woolly, regardless of how long you cook it for.

Here the method employs a roasting chicken that is effectively pot-roasted – you can use stock cubes for the initial stock. The chicken is carved up and served alongside the vegetables, while the resulting liquor, of which there will be a goodly pool left over, can be added to a new stockpot using the carcass. So it's a dish with two lives, or at least a particularly fine stock at the very end. It's simple and nurturing, the sort of soup my family insists I take them in bed when they are laid up with any sort of bug, with some very thin toast. Whatever bread you do serve, a good salty butter will be delicious slathered over it.

Serves 4–6

1 x 1.6kg free-range chicken
groundnut oil, for brushing
sea salt, black pepper
4 slender carrots, trimmed and peeled,
  halved if long
2 leeks, trimmed and thickly sliced
1 celery heart, trimmed and thickly sliced
  on the diagonal

4 garlic cloves, peeled
150ml white wine
1.5 litres chicken stock
1 bay leaf
a few sprigs of thyme
coarsely chopped flat-leaf parsley, to serve

Heat a large frying pan over a medium-high heat. Lightly coat the chicken all over with oil and season with salt and pepper. Sear the chicken on all sides to colour it, and then place it in a large casserole. Put in all the remaining ingredients, except for the parsley, so that the liquid covers the chicken by about two-thirds. Bring to the boil, and then cover and cook over a low heat for 55 minutes.

Lift out the bird and transfer to a warm plate to rest for 15–20 minutes, tipping the juices inside back into the pan. Turn the heat up to high and boil the liquor to concentrate its flavour until it is reduced by about a quarter. Skim off any scum as it rises to the surface and take out the herbs. Carve the chicken and serve with the vegetables and a little soup, scattered with parsley. Use the leftover liquid and the carcass to start a second stock.

Spicy coconut chicken soup

This soup has many ingredients in common with the Chicken mulligatawny (see page 112), but it is lighter – more of a coconut broth with a few veggies and shreds of chicken.

Serves 4

2 garlic cloves, peeled

1 teaspoon finely chopped medium-hot red chilli

2cm knob of fresh root ginger, peeled and coarsely chopped

2 tablespoons groundnut oil

3 shallots, peeled and finely sliced

2 medium carrots, trimmed, peeled and finely sliced

1 x 400ml tin of coconut milk

600ml fresh chicken stock

2 skinless free-range chicken breasts

2 tablespoons fish sauce

a couple of squeezes of lemon or lime juice

½ teaspoon caster sugar

2 spring onions, trimmed and finely sliced

coarsely chopped coriander, to serve

Place the garlic, chilli and ginger in a small blender such as a coffee grinder and reduce to a paste. Heat the oil in a medium saucepan over a medium heat, add the paste and fry it momentarily to release all the flavours. Quickly put in the shallots and carrots and fry for a couple of minutes, stirring frequently, until nice and glossy. Pour in the coconut milk and the chicken stock, bring to the boil and simmer over a low heat for 10 minutes.

Meanwhile, prepare the chicken. Cut out and discard the white tendon on the underside of each chicken breast, and then cut into thin strips. Add the chicken to the soup and simmer for 2 minutes. Stir in the fish sauce, the lemon or lime juice and the sugar. Ladle the soup into small deep bowls, piling the chicken and vegetables in the centre. Scatter over some spring onion and coriander to serve.

Chicken noodle soup

This is the classic chicken noodle soup, almost worth developing a cold for the treat of supping it propped up in bed, it's the great restorative. If vermicelli soup noodles prove elusive, gently crush vermicelli nests between your fingers to break them up. Otherwise there are all manner of tiny soup pastas that will provide the right degree of comfort.

Serves 4

25g unsalted butter
3 leeks, trimmed and thinly sliced
150ml white wine
1.2 litres fresh chicken stock
sea salt, black pepper

60g short vermicelli or other soup noodles
2 skinless free-range chicken breasts
1 tablespoon extra virgin olive oil
3 tablespoons finely chopped parsley
freshly grated Parmesan, to serve

Melt the butter in a medium saucepan over a lowish heat and fry the leeks for 5–7 minutes until starting to relax, stirring occasionally. Add the wine, turn the heat up and cook to reduce it by half. Pour in the chicken stock, season and bring to the boil. Simmer over a low heat for 10 minutes, stirring in the vermicelli soup noodles halfway through – if you are using a different type of soup pasta then adjust the cooking time accordingly, bearing in mind they should be lovely and soft rather than al dente.

While the soup base is cooking, prepare the chicken. Cut out the tendon from the lower side of the fillets and slice them into two thin escalopes. Now slice across into thin strips. Heat the olive oil in a large frying pan over a medium-high heat, add the chicken and fry for a minute or two to seal it, stirring frequently. Turn the heat up and fry for a few minutes longer until starting to colour, seasoning towards the end of cooking.

To serve, stir the parsley and chicken into the soup, taste for seasoning and ladle into warm bowls. Accompany with grated Parmesan.

The Grocer

Any shop that makes a virtue out of selling lentils, dried beans, rice and pasta is to be cherished. I can lose myself for hours among the shelves of an old-fashioned grocer, wondering at the oddities and the packaging, strange tins and jars, cloth bags sewn at the seams, with the same wonder as peering into a doll's house as a child. Grocers are for exploring, they offer insight into the culture at hand, be it Greek, Chinese, Italian or Iranian, and make for delightful shopping, providing the wherewithall for the most nurturing soups of all. I have not tried to hide my love of lentil and other bean soups in what follows, I could happily make and eat these ad infinitum.

Middle Eastern lentil soup with pomegranate syrup

Serves 6

4 tablespoons extra virgin olive oil, plus extra to serve

4 medium carrots, trimmed, peeled and finely chopped

1 celery heart, trimmed and finely sliced

2 medium onions, peeled and finely chopped

6 garlic cloves, peeled and finely chopped

1 tablespoon coarsely crushed coriander seeds

¼ teaspoon crushed chilli flakes

225g red lentils

225g yellow split peas

2 litres chicken or vegetable stock, or water

sea salt

pomegranate syrup (or lemon juice), and coarsely chopped coriander, to serve

Heat the olive oil in a large saucepan over a medium-low heat. Add the carrot, celery, onion and garlic and fry for 15–20 minutes until soft and aromatic, stirring occasionally. Stir in the crushed coriander seeds and chilli. Rinse the lentils and split peas in a sieve under the cold tap, add them to the pan and cook for 4–5 minutes, stirring occasionally. Pour in the stock or water, bring to the boil and simmer over a low heat for 1 hour – by which time the split peas should be nice and mushy. Season to taste with salt.

Ladle the soup into warmed bowls. To serve, drizzle a little pomegranate syrup over each serving, then some olive oil and finally scatter with plenty of chopped coriander.

Very Monterey soup

This one ticks all the earth mother boxes, none of which have changed since Scott McKenzie suggested you needed to wear flowers in your hair if you were going to San Francisco. A smooth red lentil soup, as good for weaning babies as for comforting older generations, most of whom hung up their sandals long ago.

Serves 6

4 tablespoons extra virgin olive oil

2 leeks, trimmed and sliced

4 medium carrots, trimmed, peeled and sliced

1 celery heart, trimmed and sliced

1 heaped tablespoon finely chopped fresh root ginger

1 heaped teaspoon finely chopped medium-hot red chilli

4 garlic cloves, peeled and finely chopped

500g red lentils, rinsed

3 tablespoons cider vinegar

2 litres chicken or vegetable stock

sea salt

Greek or sheep's milk yogurt and coarsely chopped flat-leaf parsley, to serve

Heat the olive oil in a large saucepan over a medium heat, add the leeks, carrots, celery, ginger and chilli and fry for about 10 minutes until softened and starting to colour, then add the garlic and cook for a few minutes longer. Stir in the lentils, add the cider vinegar, pour in the stock and season with salt. Bring to the boil, skim off any surface foam and simmer for 30 minutes or until the lentils are tender. Purée in batches in a liquidiser, and then taste for seasoning. Serve with a dollop of yogurt and lots of parsley.

Pomegranate syrup is lovely stuff, it performs the same tricks as balsamic vinegar without the price tag. Here a succinct drizzle works its sweet and sour magic with some chopped coriander, which is ever a breath of fresh air.

Spicy red lentil soup with garlic raita

The garlic *raita*? Well that ensures that nothing is left to chance, though in truth you don't have to go the whole hog of roasting a head of garlic – the yogurt on its own will do. I frequently have a tub of *tzatziki* in the fridge, a great low-fat snack standby, and that would work equally well here.

Serves 4

40g unsalted butter
2 garlic cloves, peeled and finely chopped
1 heaped teaspoon finely chopped fresh
  root ginger
350g leeks (trimmed weight), sliced
250g red lentils, rinsed
300g ripe tomatoes, skinned (see page 134)
  and chopped
2 whole medium-hot red chillies

1 heaped teaspoon ground cumin
1 heaped teaspoon ground coriander
¼ teaspoon turmeric
1½ teaspoons sea salt
1 tablespoon lemon or lime juice
coarsely chopped coriander, to serve

Raita
1 large head of garlic
5 tablespoons Greek yogurt

Start with the *raita*. Heat the oven to 180°C fan oven/200°C electric oven. Slice the top off the head of garlic, wrap it in foil and roast for 20–30 minutes, then allow it to cool.

While the garlic for the *raita* is roasting, make the soup. Melt the butter in a large saucepan, add the finely chopped fresh garlic, the ginger and the sliced leeks and fry over a low heat for several minutes without colouring. Add the lentils, tomatoes, chillies, spices, salt and 1.8 litres water. Bring to the boil, skim off any surface foam and simmer for 30–40 minutes, stirring occasionally. Add the lemon or lime juice, discard the chillies and taste for seasoning.

While the soup is cooking, finish making the *raita*. Squeeze the cooked inside of the roasted garlic into a bowl and mash it with the Greek yogurt and a little salt. Ladle the hot soup into warm bowls and serve with a dollop of *raita* and plenty of chopped coriander scattered over.

Lentils are at their best married with lots of aromatics, they're a great vehicle for carrying spices, garlic, chilli, lemon and the like. They provide a base note within a soup, and their mealy texture contrasts really well with silky vegetables like tomatoes and leeks.

Nada's Syrian grain soup

This healthy and nourishing soup derives from a friend Nada Saleh's book *Seductive Flavours of the Levant*, a tour of the home cooking of Lebanon, Syria and Turkey. I love the combination of lentils, rice and bulgar – far from being over-carbed, each ingredient brings a different texture and flavour to the soup, and the method itself is unusual. All the interest is added at the end rather than at the beginning, a departure from how we tend to approach soups.

Serves 4

225g red lentils, rinsed
85g short-grain rice, rinsed
85g coarse bulgar wheat
sea salt

4 tablespoons extra virgin olive oil,
   plus extra to serve
2 medium onions, peeled, halved and finely sliced
1 teaspoon ground cumin
½ lemon

Combine the lentils, rice, bulgar wheat and 2 litres water in a medium saucepan. Bring to the boil over a high heat, skim any foam from the surface, and then reduce the heat to medium. Sprinkle over 2 teaspoons of salt, half cover with a lid and simmer for 15 minutes or until the grains are tender.

Meanwhile, heat the oil in a large frying pan over a medium heat until hot but not smoking. Add the onions and fry for about 15 minutes until golden brown, stirring occasionally.

Stir the fried onions and cumin into the soup, taste for seasoning and serve in warm bowls with a little lemon juice squeezed over and a drizzle of oil. Serve with crusty bread and a side dish of spring onions, mint and olives if you wish (see below).

Syrian meze

On the side

8 spring onions, trimmed
a handful of mint leaves
50g green olives

crusty white bread, to serve 4
extra virgin olive oil

Arrange the spring onions, mint and olives in piles on a plate, with the bread and oil separately. Allow everyone to help themselves, dipping the bread in the oil and eating it with the onions, mint and olives.

The Grocer

Wintery spelt soup

I feel like PR Central for this ancient grain, and can't get enough of it, so if you are as yet unfamiliar let me convert you. It is thought to be a hybrid of emmer wheat and goat's grass, that is, it preceded modern bread wheat on which count it has a loyal following among those who suffer wheat intolerance. It does contain gluten, but spelt has a different structure that many find easier to digest.

My own appreciation, however, lies in the eating. Spelt is positively suave, which isn't always a word I associate with grains, more Tom Ford than Gerard Départieu. It also has one up on faro, with which it is often confused, as it doesn't require soaking. Not dissimilar to barley either, but spelt is tender in under 20 minutes.

Here it is woven into a wintery bowl of goodness with bacon, cabbage, a hint of chilli and lots of parsley. But give it a go in other soups with vegetables like butternut squash and red onion, long-stem broccoli and broad beans – and it laps up olive oil, garlic, spices and other leafy herbs, such as coriander and mint.

Serves 4

2 tablespoons extra virgin olive oil
150g rindless unsmoked pancetta
   or streaky bacon, diced
3 garlic cloves, peeled and finely chopped
1 teaspoon finely sliced medium-hot red chilli
2 ripe tomatoes, skinned (see page 134)
   and chopped
120g pearled spelt, rinsed

1.1 litres chicken or vegetable stock
½ small Savoy cabbage (about 300g), cut into
   wide strips with tough white parts discarded
6 tablespoons coarsely chopped flat-leaf parsley,
   plus extra to serve
sea salt
freshly grated Parmesan, to serve

Heat the olive oil in a large saucepan over a medium heat, add the pancetta or bacon and fry for 5–8 minutes until lightly golden, stirring occasionally. Add the garlic and chilli and cook for a minute until fragrant. Add the tomatoes and cook for a few minutes until mushy, then stir in the spelt. Add the stock, bring to the boil and simmer for 15 minutes, then stir in the cabbage and cook for 5 minutes more. Stir in the parsley and taste for salt. Serve with extra parsley scattered over, accompanied by the Parmesan.

Puy lentil, spinach and bacon soup

Serves 6

200g Puy lentils
500g ripe tomatoes on the vine
1 tablespoon extra virgin olive oil, plus extra to serve
150g rindless unsmoked streaky bacon, diced, or lardons
2 medium red onions, peeled and chopped
4 garlic cloves, peeled and finely chopped
150ml white wine
400g baby spinach
500ml chicken or vegetable stock
sea salt, black pepper
6 tablespoons coarsely chopped flat-leaf parsley

Bring a large pan of water to the boil, add the lentils and simmer for 20–30 minutes or until tender, then drain them into a sieve. At the same time, bring a medium pan of water to the boil, cut out a cone from the top of each tomato, plunge into the boiling water for about 20 seconds, and then into cold water. Slip off the skins and coarsely chop the flesh.

Heat a tablespoon of olive oil in a large saucepan over a medium heat, add the bacon and fry for 7–8 minutes until golden, stirring occasionally. Transfer to a bowl using a slotted spoon. Add the onion and fry for 10–15 minutes until softened and lightly golden, stirring frequently. Add the garlic and fry for a couple of minutes, and then return the bacon to the pan. Stir in the tomatoes and cook for 3–5 minutes until they collapse. Add the wine and simmer to reduce it by half.

Add the spinach, turn up the heat and cook until it wilts, stirring occasionally. Stir in the cooked lentils, add the stock and plenty of seasoning and bring to the boil, then stir in the parsley. The soup can be made in advance and gently reheated, although you will lose the vibrant green of the spinach. Serve with a few goat's cheese toasties, either on the side or floating in the soup, if you wish (see below).

On the side

Goat's cheese toasties

A little button flavoured with rosemary, juniper berries and chilli, a 'Nut Knowle', would be particularly delicious here.

12 thin slices of baguette
180–200g medium-mature goat's cheese, thinly sliced
extra virgin olive oil, to drizzle

Shortly before serving, heat the grill. Arrange the slices of baguette on a baking tray, lay the goat's cheese on top, drizzle with oil and grill until golden and crusty.

This is on the brothy side compared to soups based on red lentils or yellow split peas, both of which simmer down to a purée. Puy lentils hold their shape and this can be put to good use, it allows for crisp little croutons floating in their midst.

French green lentil soup with Roquefort

On the shopping front, green lentils carry with them unnecessary complications. Le Puy lentils are both green and French, and yet we refer to the softer mealy green lentils as 'French green lentils'. They are really quite different, the latter are softer, while Le Puy lentils are small, composed little peas by comparison. This soup plays on the success of 'peas 'n ham' and it is the good old-fashioned type that is called for.

Serves 4

1 tablespoon groundnut oil
100g unsmoked streaky bacon, diced
2 medium onions, peeled, halved and sliced
2 garlic cloves, peeled and finely chopped
200ml red wine
200g French green lentils, rinsed
1 bay leaf

1 dried red chilli, finely chopped
1.4 litres chicken stock
sea salt

Roquefort Cream
80g Roquefort, crumbled
80g crème fraîche
Tabasco

Heat the oil in a large saucepan over a medium heat, add the bacon and the onion and cook for 12–15 minutes until lightly caramelised, adding the garlic just before the end. Add the red wine and cook right down until syrupy. Add the lentils, the bay leaf, the chilli and the chicken stock. Bring to a simmer and cook for 40 minutes. Season generously with salt.

While the soup is cooking, mash the Roquefort and crème fraîche together in a bowl and season with a dash of Tabasco. Serve the soup in warm bowls, with a spoon of the Roquefort cream in the middle.

Quick fasolada

This bean soup is one of the national treasures of the Greek table, and very much quicker to prepare if you cheat with tinned white beans and chopped tomatoes. It will be just as colourful as if you had slaved over it for hours, and there's little that a good olive oil won't sort out, poured over at the end.

Serves 4

4 tablespoons extra virgin olive oil, plus extra
    to serve
1 medium onion, peeled and chopped
4 medium carrots, trimmed, peeled, halved
    lengthways and thinly sliced
1 celery heart, trimmed and thinly sliced
3 garlic cloves, peeled and finely chopped

3 x 300g or 2 x 400g tins of cannellini or other
    white beans, drained
1 x 400g tin of chopped tomatoes
1 litre vegetable or chicken stock
sea salt, black pepper
6 tablespoons coarsely chopped flat-leaf parsley

Heat 4 tablespoons oil in a large saucepan over a medium-low heat and fry the onion, carrot and celery for about 20 minutes until glossy and softened, adding the garlic just before the end. Add the drained beans and give them a stir, then the tomatoes, stock and some seasoning. Bring to the boil and simmer for 15 minutes. Stir in the parsley, taste to check the seasoning and serve with plenty of olive oil poured over.

Two-lentil soup
with caramelised onions and lemon

When I first ate this soup at a café in Camden (sadly now closed), it was a revelation. The soup itself was relatively dull, but smothered at the end with slowly caramelised onions, and with a generous squeeze of lemon juice and some olive oil, it was fab. You don't have to weave all the interest into a soup as it simmers – by adding grace notes at the end you frequently get a livelier result than simply trying to trick up the broth with more of this or that, the danger of course being that you go on adding salt. Here the onions take a little time, and there are quicker options – for example, a sprinkling of chopped fresh parsley or coriander, along with a good spritz of lemon juice and olive oil.

Serves 4–6

4 tablespoons extra virgin olive oil
4 medium carrots, trimmed, peeled and sliced
1 celery heart, trimmed and sliced
2 medium red onions, peeled and chopped
5cm knob of fresh root ginger, peeled and
    finely chopped
6 garlic cloves, peeled and finely chopped
225g red lentils
225g yellow split peas

2 litres vegetable stock
sea salt, black pepper
To serve
2 tablespoons extra virgin olive oil, plus extra
    for drizzling
2 large onions (ideally white), peeled, halved and
    sliced as finely as possible
4 squeezes of lemon juice

Heat the olive oil for the soup in a large saucepan over a medium-low heat, add the carrot, celery, red onion, ginger and garlic and fry, stirring occasionally, for about 20 minutes until soft and aromatic. Rinse the lentils and split peas in a sieve under the cold tap, and then add them to the pan. Cook for 4–5 minutes, stirring occasionally. Pour in the vegetable stock, bring to the boil and simmer over a low heat for 1 hour – by which time the split peas should be nice and mushy.

While the soup is cooking, heat 2 tablespoons olive oil in a large frying pan over a very low heat. Add the finely sliced onions and cook for 40–50 minutes, stirring frequently, especially towards the end when they are more liable to catch and burn. By the end, they should be a deep even gold. Transfer to a bowl.

Liquidise the soup in batches with some salt and pepper – it should be very thick, the consistency of a thin purée. Ladle it into warmed soup bowls, squeeze a little lemon juice over each serving and drizzle with some olive oil. Finally strew over the caramelised onions.

The Grocer

Plum tomato soup with green lentils

Many of my favourite lentil soups are the sort that carry you from lunch to supper without a further pang of hunger. But this soup is an exception. Here the French green lentils play only a small part, just a few in a tomato soup pepped up with chilli, and lots of parsley stirred in at the end. Light enough to provide us with an excuse for tea, unless you take into account the marinated prawns suggested as an aside.

Serves 4

6 tablespoons extra virgin olive oil, plus extra to serve

2 medium onions, peeled and chopped

2 medium carrots, trimmed, peeled and thinly sliced

2 sticks of celery heart, trimmed and thinly sliced

1 heaped teaspoon finely chopped medium-hot red chilli

4 garlic cloves, peeled and finely chopped

1.5kg ripe beefsteak or plum tomatoes

100g French green lentils, rinsed

a pinch of saffron filaments (about 20)

1 teaspoon caster sugar

sea salt

6 tablespoons coarsely chopped flat-leaf parsley

Heat 3 tablespoons olive oil in a large saucepan over a medium heat and fry the onion, carrot, celery and chilli for 10–15 minutes, stirring frequently, until lightly coloured, adding the garlic halfway through.
At the same time, bring a medium pan of water to the boil, cut out a small cone from the top of each tomato to remove the core, and then plunge them into the boiling water for about 20 seconds (you may need to do this in batches). Immediately transfer them to a bowl of cold water, and then slip off the skins and coarsely chop the flesh.

Add the tomatoes, lentils, saffron, sugar and 400ml water to the vegetables and bring to the boil. Cover and cook over a low heat for 35–40 minutes until the lentils are tender. Season the soup with salt, and add half the parsley and 3 tablespoons of olive oil. Serve in warm bowls, drizzled with a little extra oil and scattered with the rest of the parsley. Accompany with the prawn brochettes if you wish (see below).

On the side ## Prawn brochettes

200g shelled raw king prawns (ideally tail-on)

2cm knob of fresh root ginger, peeled and coarsely grated

2 garlic cloves, peeled and crushed to a paste

2 tablespoons extra virgin olive oil

sea salt, black pepper

¼ lemon

Thread the prawns onto four 15cm skewers. Blend the ginger and garlic with the olive oil on a plate, or in a shallow container. Coat the prawns with the marinade, and then cover and chill for a couple of hours (ideally overnight), but if you are in a rush you can grill them straight away.

Heat a ridged griddle, season the skewers and cook them for 1–2 minutes on the first side, and about 1 minute on the second. Squeeze over a little lemon juice to serve.

Scotch broth

Barley is the defining ingredient here, with its satisfyingly slippery and wholesome goodness, served in a broth sweetened by lamb and packed with nourishing, soft winter vegetables. You can dice the vegetables really quite small for this – which is the ideal, but I don't want to put you under any pressure – you can also leave them that little bit larger and provide a fork with the spoon for mashing them into the liquor as you go.

Serves 6

1 bay leaf
500g lamb neck fillet, halved lengthways and
*   sliced 1cm thick*
300g turnips, trimmed, peeled and diced
300g swede, peeled and diced
300g waxy potatoes, scrubbed or peeled
*   as necessary, and diced*
1 leek, trimmed and thinly sliced

1 celery heart, trimmed and thinly sliced
2 medium carrots, trimmed, peeled, halved
*   lengthways and sliced*
sea salt, black pepper
2 litres chicken stock
100g pearl barley
6 tablespoons coarsely chopped
*   flat-leaf parsley, to serve*

Combine all the ingredients except for the parsley in a large casserole. Bring to the boil and skim off any foam as it rises to the surface – you may need to do this a couple of times in the early stages of simmering. Cook over a low heat for 1 hour. Stir in the parsley and season to taste. The soup can be made in advance and reheated, in which case scrape off the fat on the surface once it has cooled.

Ham and barley soup with mustard cream

A great post-Christmas favourite in our house, which turns all sorts of leftover goodies into a potful of comfort. If you cooked your own ham for Christmas, the stock can be put to good use here – although depending on how salty it is, you might need to dilute it with turkey or chicken stock.

Serves 6

50g unsalted butter
1 celery heart, trimmed and sliced
2 large carrots (about 250g), trimmed, peeled
*   and thinly sliced on the diagonal*
2 leeks, trimmed and thinly sliced
75g pearl barley
2 litres ham or chicken stock

6 thin slices of ham, fat removed, cut into
*   1 x 5cm strips*
150g crème fraîche
1 tablespoon Dijon mustard
sea salt, black pepper
coarsely chopped flat-leaf parsley, to serve

Melt the butter in a large saucepan over a medium heat, add the celery, carrot and leeks and fry for 5 minutes, stirring occasionally, until glossy but not coloured. Stir in the pearl barley and fry for a minute or two, stirring. Add the stock, bring to the boil and simmer over a low heat for 30 minutes or until the barley is tender, adding the ham just before the end. Meanwhile, blend the crème fraîche and mustard in a bowl. Season the soup with black pepper and more salt if necessary. Serve in warm bowls with the mustard cream spooned in the centre, scattered with parsley.

Russian mushroom soup

There's enough Russian spirit here with wild mushrooms, dill and soured cream to conjure warmth on a cold winter's day. It can be turned into an even heartier bowlful with a pile of noodles and wild mushrooms scattered over it, or eaten on the side (see below).

You could boost the flavour further with the addition of some dried wild mushrooms. Cover 30g dried mushrooms with 300ml boiling stock (taken from the total amount) and leave to soak for 15 minutes. Add the drained mushrooms along with all of the cooked vegetables, and add the soaking liquor with the rest of the stock.

Serves 6

225g wild or interesting cultivated mushrooms (shiitake, chanterelles, girolles, etc.)
25g unsalted butter
400g white mushrooms, sliced
1 medium onion, peeled and chopped
1 leek, trimmed and sliced

1 small fennel bulb, trimmed and chopped
150ml white wine
1.35 litres chicken or vegetable stock
sea salt, black pepper
150ml double cream

Pick over all the wild mushrooms, scrape or wipe them if they are dirty and slice them if necessary.

You will need to cook the vegetables in batches to avoid overcrowding the pan. Melt the butter in a large saucepan over a medium heat and fry the mushrooms, onion, leek and fennel together until soft. If the mushrooms give out their juices, reserve these along with the cooked vegetables.

Place all the cooked vegetables back into the saucepan, add the wine and cook to reduce it by half. Add the stock and some seasoning, bring to the boil and simmer for 15 minutes. Liquidise the soup in batches and return to the pan. If you want a really smooth soup, you could liquidise it again. Stir in the double cream. The soup can be made to this point in advance.

Close to the time of serving, reheat the soup if necessary, ladle into warm bowls and serve with the Mushroom noodles (see below) if wished.

On the side ## Mushroom noodles

100g thin egg noodles
25g unsalted butter
2 shallots, peeled and finely chopped
225g wild mushrooms (prepared as above)

sea salt, black pepper
a squeeze of lemon juice
150ml soured cream
snipped dill

Bring a pan of salted water to the boil. Add the noodles, stir to separate them and cook until tender, leaving them firm to the bite. Drain and reserve in a sieve. Melt the butter in a large frying pan over a medium-high heat and fry the shallot for a minute or two. Add the mushrooms and toss until they soften, then season with salt, pepper and a squeeze of lemon juice. Add the noodles to the pan and gently heat together, tasting for seasoning. Pile the mushroom noodles in the centre of the soup, drizzle over some soured cream and scatter with the snipped dill.

Pistou

A great heatwave soup, for those rare days when it's so hot you plan to get everything including the cooking out of the way before mid-morning. Then you can settle down to a leisurely lunch of newly cooled *pistou* with a bottle of chilled rosé before retiring for a siesta.

Serves 4

1 litre vegetable stock or water
500g mixed green summer vegetables, diced
   or sliced, e.g. courgette, French beans,
   celery heart
50g short vermicelli or other soup noodles
   (see page 124)

2 x 300g tins of flageolet beans, drained
   and rinsed
40g basil leaves
125g freshly grated Parmesan
4 garlic cloves, peeled
75ml extra virgin olive oil, plus extra to serve
   sea salt, black pepper

Bring the stock or water to the boil, add the vegetables and soup noodles and simmer for 10 minutes, adding the flageolet beans just before the end. Whizz the basil, Parmesan, garlic and olive oil in a food processor and stir into the cooked soup, then season to taste. Serve with a little more oil drizzled over.

Speedy chickpea and cabbage soup

I have only ever had variable success at ridding dried chickpeas of their chalky heart – something that has everything to do with how fresh they are. Tinned pulses are a guarantee of tenderness.

Serves 4

60g unsalted butter
2 medium onions, peeled and chopped
1 celery heart, trimmed and sliced
3 garlic cloves, peeled and finely chopped
1 teaspoon turmeric
1 teaspoon ground cumin
a large pinch of cayenne pepper

2 x 400g tins of chickpeas, plus 1 x 200g tin,
   drained and rinsed
700ml vegetable stock
1½ teaspoons sea salt
1–2 tablespoons lemon juice
70g green cabbage leaves

Melt 40g butter in a large saucepan over a medium heat and fry the onion and celery for about 5 minutes until softened, stirring occasionally. Stir in the garlic and spices and cook for 1 minute. Stir in the two 400g tins of chickpeas, add the stock and salt and bring to the boil. Simmer for 5 minutes, and then liquidise in a blender with a tablespoon of lemon juice. If you are making it in advance, you may need to thin the soup with a little more stock before serving.

At the same time as cooking the soup, bring a medium pan of salted water to the boil, add the cabbage and simmer for 5 minutes, then drain and finely slice. Melt the remaining 20g butter in a large frying pan over a medium heat, add the 200g tin of chickpeas to the pan with the cabbage. Season with salt and fry for a couple of minutes. Season to taste with a squeeze of lemon juice. Ladle the soup into warm bowls and serve the cabbage and chickpea mixture spooned over the top.

Ham hock and split pea soup

In France there is a thriving tradition of artisanal producers of air-dried ham. I'm not sure why they should have all but disappeared in this country, given that ham was once a mainstay for households here in the same way as it was there. The fireplace in the kitchen of our 17th-century Norman farmhouse has endless nooks and hooks related to cooking. The mantlepiece is some six feet high, which is not unusual, and hams would have hung and dried in the recess, as they would have done in this country too.

There are still many small artisanal producers in our French neck of the woods, and one of the great joys are the cheap off-cuts of the production, namely the knuckles or uncooked ham hocks, which you can buy vac-packed with a sell-by date of several months. They are a great fallback with a packet of lentils. They need around a couple of hours cooking to render them desirably fork tender, but what a fine job they do of releasing their gelatine and flavour into the broth, and as with lamb shanks the end result is almost entirely edible save a slim bone. Most producers elsewhere will probably be very happy to supply these.

Serves 6

1 x 750g ham hock (or equivalent of smaller ones)
4 tablespoons extra virgin olive oil, plus extra to serve
4 medium carrots, trimmed, peeled and thinly sliced
1 celery heart, trimmed and thinly sliced

2 medium onions, peeled and chopped
500g yellow split peas
1 bay leaf
1 small dried red chilli, crumbled
sea salt
coarsely chopped flat-leaf parsley, to serve

Place the ham hock in a large saucepan and cover with water. Bring to the boil, and then drain and set aside. Heat the olive oil in the same saucepan over a medium-low heat, add the carrot, celery and onion, and fry for 20–25 minutes until soft and aromatic, stirring occasionally.

Rinse the split peas in a sieve under the cold tap, and add them to the pan. Add 2½ litres water, the ham hock, bay leaf and chilli. Bring to the boil, skimming in the process, and then simmer over a low heat for 1 hour. Now cover with a lid and simmer for a further hour, by which time the split peas should be nice and mushy, and the ham meltingly tender.

Remove the ham from the pan onto a plate or chopping board, peel off the rind and shred the flesh off the bone using a fork. Add this back to the pan, and season to taste with salt – remember that the stock might be quite salty already from the ham.

Serve in warm bowls splashed with oil and scattered with parsley. Although the soup sets quite solidly once cool, it can be successfully reheated.

Peas 'n rice soup

If you keep adding stock to a risotto you eventually arrive at a soup, the difference here being that you go straight to the finishing line – which does away with hovering over the pan. This dish is a real blaze of early summer, full of green goodies and lots of herbs.

Serves 4

60g unsalted butter
1 bunch of spring onions (about 6), trimmed and sliced into 1cm lengths
200g carnaroli rice
200g shelled fresh peas
200g shelled young broad beans (fresh or frozen)
150ml white wine
1.5 litres chicken stock
sea salt, black pepper
50g watercress, leaves and tender stems
50g flat-leaf parsley, leaves and tender stems
15g mint leaves
75g freshly grated Parmesan, plus a little extra to serve

Melt half the butter in a large saucepan over a medium heat and fry the spring onions for several minutes until limp and glossy. Add the rice and stir to coat it in the butter, then add the peas and broad beans and stir for about a minute. Pour in the wine and stock, and season with salt and pepper. Turn the heat up and bring to the boil, and then cover and cook over a low heat for 15 minutes – by which time the rice should be tender.

Meanwhile, heat the remaining 30g butter in a large frying pan, add the watercress and herbs and toss until they wilt. Once the soup is cooked, tip the herbs into a food processor and add a ladle of the soup stock. Reduce to a coarse purée, and then stir this back into the soup along with the Parmesan. Taste to check the seasoning before ladling into warm bowls. Scatter over a little extra Parmesan and serve. The soup will sit around for a few minutes, but is best eaten fairly quickly to capture the freshness of the herbs.

The Baker

Where would soup be without bread? It shares the stage, along with a good butter, the dipping and mopping are as soothing a ritual as the soup itself. So there is no hiding some mass-produced limp slice, that will only drag the occasion down. The art of the artisan is all here and a trip to a baker a must. We can never agree in our house whether it should be soft and white or a hearty wholegrain, which is a great excuse for buying on whimsy. And providing the white is sturdy in character, either a sourdough or a country-style loaf, then the leftover is the starting point for any number of lovely soups too. It is when a couple of days have passed and the bread is that little bit too dry to enjoy without toasting that it really comes into its own. Part of a gratifying recycling of ingredients, that is so central to soups.

Ajo blanco

White gazpacho, traditionally eaten with grapes (although it is stunning with pomegranate seeds too), is less well known than the classic garlicky chilled tomato variety – but just as traditional. Supposed to have originated with the Moors, it owes its exquisite delicacy and colour to almonds, which are sometimes soaked in milk before they are ground to soften them further.

Ultimately it is as healthy as it is simple to make, and a great storecupboard fallback. I always seem to have endless packets of almonds in the drawer, as a result of being a favourite ingredient in cakes, and the other ingredients are no more challenging to rustle up – at most a case of popping out to the corner shop for a few items. All it needs is a little rest in the fridge to chill it down and give the almonds and bread time to thicken the soup.

Serves 4

100g day-old coarse-textured white bread, torn up
200g blanched almonds
2 garlic cloves, peeled and coarsely chopped
4 tablespoons extra virgin olive oil, plus extra to serve

20ml sherry vinegar
sea salt
150ml white grape juice
halved red and white seedless grapes, to serve

Place the bread in a bowl and cover with cold water. Place the almonds in a food processor and whizz for a couple of minutes to a powdered consistency – by the end they should be sticking together. Squeeze out the bread and add to the food processor with the garlic, olive oil, vinegar, 2 teaspoons salt and a little cold water. Reduce to a creamy purée, scraping down the sides of the bowl as necessary. Slowly pour in the remainder of the water through the funnel with the motor running, and then add the grape juice. Transfer the soup to a bowl and taste to check the seasoning – it may benefit from another half a teaspoon of salt. Cover and chill for a couple of hours, during which time it will thicken a little to the consistency of single cream.

Serve the soup in bowls with a zigzag of oil drizzled over, scattered with red and white grape halves and accompanied by the smoked duck and a rocket salad (see below) if you wish.

On the side ## Smoked duck

100g sliced smoked duck

Rocket salad

50g rocket leaves
50g roasted marcona almonds

50g quince cheese or paste, sliced transparently thin
extra virgin olive oil, to drizzle

Combine the rocket leaves, roasted almonds and slivers of quince cheese on a plate, and drizzle over a little olive oil.

Gazpacho

If you have ever visited Andalucía in southern Spain during the summer months you will understand why gazpacho is so central to their culture. I recall one August staying in a flat in Seville without air-conditioning. From late morning to early evening we would sit wilting on the terrace with our hands and feet dangling in bowls of cold water, changed every half or so as they heated up. So venturing out into the relative cool of the evening air for a bowl of gazpacho soothed in a way that no other food could have done.

Take away the name and look at the ingredients, and it is basically a puréed salad, chilled. We tend to think of gazpacho as a tomato soup, but it was originally a bread soup, most likely introduced to Spain by the Moors, with the addition of olive oil, water and garlic. Tomatoes were a later addition after the discovery of the New World in the late 15th century. In fact, the Ajo blanco (see page 152) is probably much more in keeping with the original.

When tomatoes are in season during the summer months, perfectly ripe and flavourful – which sadly is the exception rather than the rule – then big misshapen old-fashioned varieties will make for a fabulous soup. At other times of the year, cherry tomatoes promise an intense sweetness and perfume, which is why I am inclined to use them as a default here. Any number of little frills can finish the soup off – seafood goes especially well, a spoon of crabmeat or a few clams – but a final splash of olive oil is hard to beat.

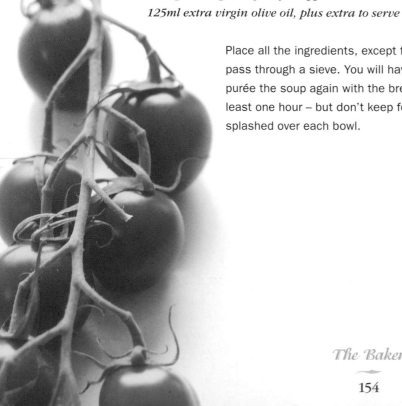

Serves 4

1.1kg ripe cherry tomatoes
1 cucumber, ends discarded, peeled and
   cut into pieces
1 garlic clove, peeled and chopped
1 heaped teaspoon medium-hot chopped fresh
   red chilli
2 heaped teaspoons finely chopped onion
125ml extra virgin olive oil, plus extra to serve

½ tablespoon red wine or sherry vinegar
2 heaped teaspoons caster sugar
2 rounded teaspoons sea salt
a grinding of black pepper
3 thick slices of day-old white bread, crusts
   removed (about 90g trimmed weight),
   broken into pieces

Place all the ingredients, except for the bread, in a blender and reduce to a purée, then pass through a sieve. You will have to do this in batches. Rinse out the blender and purée the soup again with the bread. Pour into a bowl, and then cover and chill for at least one hour – but don't keep for longer than necessary. Serve with some olive oil splashed over each bowl.

Ribollita

Only the Italians could get away with serving something as gloriously messy as this in the name of soup – the French would be appalled. The Italians have the upper hand here – such soups are nothing without their clichéd drizzling of olive oil. It's worth ignoring the price tag and investing in a bottle that gives you particular pleasure.

Serves 6

5 tablespoons extra virgin olive oil, plus
    extra to serve
1 celery heart, trimmed and thinly sliced
1 large carrot, trimmed, peeled and thinly sliced
2 leeks, trimmed and sliced
4 garlic cloves, peeled and thinly sliced
400g ripe cherry tomatoes on the vine, halved
1 x 400g tin of chopped tomatoes
1 small dried red chilli, crumbled

4 handfuls of coarsely chopped flat-leaf parsley
700ml vegetable stock
½ Savoy cabbage, core removed, quartered,
    finely sliced and halved into shorter strands
1 x 400g tin of borlotti beans, drained and rinsed
1 bay leaf
sea salt
½ ciabatta loaf (about 200g), torn into pieces
    the size of a walnut

Heat 4 tablespoons olive oil in a large saucepan over a medium heat and fry the celery, carrot, leeks and garlic for about 15 minutes until nicely golden, stirring frequently.

Add the fresh and tinned tomatoes to the pan with the chilli and half the parsley, along with another tablespoon of oil. Simmer for about 10 minutes over a low heat until well reduced. Now add the stock, cabbage, beans and bay leaf. Bring to the boil and simmer over a low heat for 10–15 minutes until the cabbage is tender. Season to taste with salt. Stir in the bread and the remaining parsley, and leave to stand for a few minutes. Serve with more olive oil poured over.

Garlic soup with a poached egg

This French classic is rustic and soul-satisfying. At its heart is a lightly poached egg on toast, soaked by a garlic-rich broth, with some strings of melted Gruyère for good measure.

Serves 4

2 heads of garlic, broken into cloves and peeled
3 sprigs of soft-leaved thyme, plus 1 heaped teaspoon thyme leaves
1 bay leaf
850ml light chicken stock
150ml dry vermouth
3 tablespoons extra virgin olive oil, plus extra for brushing
sea salt, black pepper
8 slices of baguette, 1cm thick
a slug of white wine vinegar
4 large organic eggs
150g finely grated Gruyère

Place the garlic, thyme sprigs and bay leaf in a medium saucepan with the chicken stock, vermouth, olive oil, a heaped teaspoon of sea salt and a grinding of black pepper. Bring to the boil, and then simmer over a low heat for 30 minutes. Strain the soup into a clean pan, pressing the garlic through the sieve with the back of a spoon. Add the thyme leaves and taste to check for seasoning.

While the soup is cooking, heat the oven to 180°C fan oven/200°C electric oven. Lay the slices of baguette in a baking dish and bake for 5 minutes until dried out. Remove and brush with olive oil on both sides. Return them to the oven for another 10–12 minutes until lightly golden.

Bring a large pan of water to the boil and acidulate it with a slug of vinegar. Turn the heat down low until the water is barely trembling. Stir it into a whirlpool and break in the eggs one at a time. Once they rise to the surface, trim off any ragged tails of white, and cook for about 4 minutes in total.

While the eggs are cooking, reheat the soup. Place two croutons in the base of four warmed deep soup bowls. Remove the eggs one at a time using a slotted spoon and place on top of the croutons. Ladle the soup over. Serve the cheese separately at the table.

Bacon and sage dumplings in broth

Serves 4

Dumplings
100g rindless streaky bacon, coarsely sliced
120g fresh white breadcrumbs
100g shredded suet
about 8 sage leaves, finely chopped
3 medium organic egg yolks

sea salt, black pepper
Soup
800ml chicken stock
100ml white wine
coarsely chopped flat-leaf parsley and freshly
   grated Parmesan, to serve

Place the bacon in the bowl of a food processor and finely chop it. Add the breadcrumbs, suet, sage, egg yolks and some seasoning and whizz until the mixture looks sticky. Keeping the motor running, add just enough water for the dough to start to cling together in lumps. Shape the dough into balls the size of a cherry and place on a plate. Cover and chill if you are not cooking them in the near future.

To cook the dumplings, bring the stock and wine to the boil with a little salt in a large saucepan and simmer over a low heat for 15 minutes. Add the dumplings and poach over a low heat for 10 minutes. Ladle into bowls and serve scattered with parsley, and lots of Parmesan.

Turkish village soup with bread and caraway

From Sam and Sam Clark's cookbook *Casa Moro*, which explores the cooking of Spain and the Muslim Mediterranean. Try to cook your own beans – they are a world apart from tinned in this recipe.

Serves 4

8 tablespoons extra virgin olive oil,
   plus extra to serve
1 large onion, finely chopped
3 large carrots, trimmed, peeled and finely
   chopped
4 celery sticks, finely chopped
sea salt, black pepper
4 garlic cloves, peeled and thinly sliced
3 level teaspoons caraway seeds
3 tablespoons coarsely chopped flat-leaf parsley

1 x 400g tin of whole plum tomatoes,
   drained of juice and broken up
500g white cabbage, thinly sliced and chopped
1.25 litres water (or 1 litre water and 250ml
   bean liquor)
400g cooked borlotti or pinto beans (200g dried
   weight), or 2 x 400g tins
200g day-old ciabatta or sourdough bread
   (crusts removed), torn into bite-sized pieces

Heat the olive oil in a large saucepan over a medium heat, add the onion, carrot, celery and a pinch of salt and gently fry for 15–20 minutes until the vegetables begin to turn golden, stirring occasionally. Add the garlic, caraway and half the parsley and fry for 1–2 minutes, then add the tomatoes. Cook for another 5–8 minutes, again stirring occasionally. Add the cabbage and water (or water and bean liquor) and bring to the boil. Simmer over a low heat for 20 minutes until the cabbage is almost cooked. Add the beans and simmer for a further 10 minutes until the cabbage is tender, stirring frequently.

Remove from heat, the taste for seasoning, then stir in the bread and the rest of the parsley. Leave to stand for 5 minutes. If it is too dry, add a little more liquid. Serve drizzled with extra virgin olive oil.

Here the soup plays second fiddle to the bacon dumplings, which are especially comforting eased down by a thin broth. With Parmesan and parsley in there too, this need be no more than a decent homemade stock.

Oven-baked French onion soup

This takes a French onion soup to its logical extreme. This is as much to do with the croutons and molten cheese as it is with any liquid. Here they are layered with just a few onions with just enough stock to cover.

Serves 4

50g unsalted butter

3 medium onions, peeled, halved and thinly sliced

150ml white wine

1 litre chicken or beef stock

sea salt, black pepper

2 tablespoons brandy

5–6 slices of sourdough bread, from a small loaf, toasted

200g grated Beaufort

Melt the butter in a large saucepan over a medium heat and fry the onions for 20–30 minutes until they are a deep even gold, stirring frequently. It's really important to take your time here and not rush them. Add the wine and simmer until well reduced, then add the chicken stock and some seasoning. Bring to the boil and simmer over a low heat for 10 minutes. Stir in the brandy. The soup can be made well in advance.

Heat the oven to 220°C fan oven/240°C electric oven. Pour about a quarter of the hot soup over the base of a large casserole. Lay 2–3 slices of toast on top and pile on half the cheese. Ladle over two-thirds of the remaining soup and repeat with the rest of the ingredients. Place in the oven for 15 minutes until the cheese and toast on top are golden and sizzling. Serve straight away.

Beans on toast soup

The charm is in the comforting double whammy of carbs – here creamy haricot beans with thick slabs of toast, soaked in a light broth sharpened with tomatoes. A shower of Parmesan or Pecorino is always good.

Serves 6

2 tablespoons extra virgin olive oil, plus extra to serve

1 onion, peeled and finely chopped

2 shallots, peeled and finely chopped

1 garlic clove, peeled and finely chopped

1 celery heart, thinly sliced

1 tablespoon thyme leaves

1 x 400g tin of chopped tomatoes

300g dried haricot beans, soaked overnight

200g ripe cherry tomatoes on the vine, halved

1 small dried red chilli, crumbled

1.4 litres chicken or vegetable stock

sea salt

6 thick slices of day-old sourdough bread, toasted

freshly grated Parmesan or Pecorino, to serve

Heat the olive oil in a large saucepan over a medium-low heat and fry the onion, shallot, garlic, celery and thyme for 5–10 minutes until nice and soft, without allowing the vegetables to colour. Add the tinned tomatoes and simmer until well reduced. Put in the soaked haricot beans, cherry tomatoes, chilli and stock and bring to the boil. Skim off any foam and simmer over a low heat for 1¼ hours or until the beans are meltingly tender. Season with a little salt.

To serve, reheat the soup if necessary and ladle over thick slices of toast drizzled with oil. Finish with a final drizzle of oil and accompany with grated Parmesan or Pecorino.

Pappa al pomodoro

Should you find yourself in Umbria during the summer, this tomato and bread soup seems like such an obvious dish to make with the proceeds of a morning's shopping. You can leave the tomatoes in the sun to soften and draw out their sweetness and juices while you enjoy a pre-prandial drink, and you'll be pleased to discover the rather hard unsalted bread that might have seemed like a challenge at breakfast holds its own in a liquid medium.

Serves 4

1.5kg ripe beefsteak tomatoes
8 tablespoons extra virgin olive oil
3 garlic cloves, peeled and finely chopped
1 teaspoon caster sugar

sea salt
2 handfuls of basil leaves, torn
4 thick slices of slightly stale coarse-textured
    white bread

Bring a large pan of water to the boil, cut out a cone from the top of each tomato and plunge them into boiling water for about 20 seconds – you may need to do this in batches. Transfer them to a bowl of cold water, slip off the skins and coarsely chop the flesh.

Heat half the olive oil in a medium or large saucepan over a medium heat, add the garlic and cook for a minute or two until it starts to colour. Tip in the tomatoes and add the sugar and some salt. Give everything a stir, put on a lid and simmer over a low heat for 15–20 minutes until softened and soupy.

Add 100ml water, the basil and the remaining olive oil and gently heat through. Meanwhile, toast the bread. Ladle the soup over the bread in shallow bowls, and serve with a plate of antipasti (see below) on the side if you wish.

On the side ## Antipasti

4 slices air-dried ham
75g black olives
1 x 125g buffalo mozzarella, cut into wedges

Arrange the ham, olives and mozzarella in piles on a plate or board.

Bread sides

Especially crispy croutons

These crisp golden croutons are a classic for scattering over pretty much any soup.

day-old white bread, cut into slices 1cm thick

groundnut oil, for shallow frying

Cut the crusts off the bread and dice it, using a sharp chopping knife rather than a bread knife which will tear the crumb. Heat several millimetres of oil in a frying pan until it is hot enough to immerse a cube of bread in bubbles. Add a single layer of croutons to the pan and fry them, tossing occasionally until they are evenly gold and crisp. Remove them with a slotted spoon and drain on kitchen paper. Leave to cool. These croutons are at their best the day they are made.

Oregano croutons

These oven-baked croutons are a little lighter on the oil than the above, and flavoured with dried oregano.

100g day-old white bread (crusts removed), cut into 1cm dice

3 tablespoons extra virgin olive oil

1 heaped teaspoon dried oregano

Heat the oven to 180°C fan oven/200°C electric oven. Toss the bread in a large bowl with the olive oil and the oregano. Spread the croutons on a baking tray and bake for 12–15 minutes until golden. Leave to cool.

Plain garlic bread

It's hard to beat garlic bread made with Breton or Normandy butter laced with sea salt crystals, good plump cloves of garlic and a well-crafted baguette.

50g softened Breton or Normandy salted butter

2–3 garlic cloves, peeled and crushed to a paste

small baguette

Blend the butter with the crushed garlic. Thickly slice the baguette, leaving the pieces attached at the base, and generously spread either side of each slice with garlic butter. Alternatively, slit the baguette in half lengthways and spread top and bottom. Wrap in foil and bake for 15 minutes at 180°C fan oven/200°C electric oven. Open up the foil and cook for a further 5 minutes to crisp the crust.

Slightly more sophisticated herby garlic bread

A little less heady than the above, with lots of herbs to enhance the experience.

50g softened Breton or Normandy salted butter

6 tablespoons chopped soft herbs (e.g. parsley, chives, chervil, coriander and/or tarragon)

1 garlic clove, peeled and crushed to a paste

small baguette

Blend the butter with the herbs and garlic. Prepare and cook as for the Plain garlic bread above.

Rarebits

Mini rarebits are great with any number of soups, but especially those in the Greengrocer chapter, and lentil ones too. Or you could make them larger and pile a mustardy green salad on top to follow the soup, which turns it into a more complete repast.

Serves 6

6 slices day-old white bread
Rarebit mixture
30g day-old white bread (crusts removed)
250g mature Cheddar, cut into chunks
30g unsalted butter

3 tablespoons stout
1 teaspoon Dijon mustard
1 teaspoon Worcestershire sauce
1 medium organic egg

Place the bread for the rarebit mixture in the bowl of a food processor and whizz to crumbs. Add all the remaining ingredients for the mixture and blend to a paste. You can make this well in advance, in which case transfer it to a bowl, cover and chill it.

Toast the bread and cut into triangles or smaller pieces, leaving the crusts on. Spread thickly with the rarebit mixture and place on a grill tray. You will need to grill them under a lowish heat to cook the inside of the mixture – either under a medium heat for 5–7 minutes, or a low heat for about 5 minutes – turning it up to brown the top.

Pitta toasts

Things on toast are always a good way of spinning out a bowl of soup. Here, if you can run to all three suggestions it will make for an elegant lunch.

Slit two pitta breads in half using a sharp knife, and toast them on either side under a grill. Cut each piece into three or four strips.

Paprika, thyme and olive oil

Drizzle *a little olive oil* over the toasts, dust with *paprika* and sprinkle with *thyme leaves*.

Feta and dill

Mash *200g feta cheese* in a bowl with *3 tablespoons extra virgin olive oil* and *a tablespoon of chopped dill*. Pile this mixture onto the toasts and drizzle with a little more olive oil. You can serve these cold, or toast them under the grill until the cheese is soft and starting to colour.

Pea and chorizo

Simmer *200g fresh or frozen peas* in boiling water for 2–3 minutes or until tender; drain. Whizz to a coarse purée in a food processor with *4 tablespoons olive oil*, *a little salt* and *a squeeze of lemon juice*. Transfer the mixture to a bowl and stir in *1–2 finely sliced spring onions*, and *25g sliced chorizo*, cut into thin strips. Pile this onto the toasts and drizzle with a little more olive oil.

Cocktail shortbreads

One dough, three types of biscuit. These are a good way of turning a relatively plain bowl of soup into something more elaborate.

Serves 10

Dough
- *150g plain flour*
- *75g ground almonds*
- *150g salted butter (e.g. Brittany butter), chilled and diced*

Flavourings
- *1 heaped teaspoon poppy seeds, plus extra for rolling*
- *finely grated zest of 1 lemon*
- *1 heaped teaspoon sesame seeds, plus extra for rolling*
- *½ teaspoon ground cumin*
- *25g freshly grated Parmesan*
- *cayenne pepper*
- *vegetable oil, for brushing*

Place the flour, ground almonds and butter in the bowl of a food processor and briefly whizz to fine crumbs – it's important to heed the 'briefly' here otherwise you'll end up with a dough.

Divide the mixture between three bowls. Stir a heaped teaspoon of poppy seeds and the lemon zest into one bowl, a heaped teaspoon of sesame seeds and the ground cumin into the other, and the Parmesan and a suspicion of cayenne pepper into the third bowl. Bring each mixture together into a ball using your hands.

Form the cheese dough into a rough sausage shape about 3cm in diameter, wrap in clingfilm and give it a roll to smooth it out. Wrap the remaining two balls of dough in clingfilm. You can freeze the doughs at this point, otherwise chill them all for an hour or two.

Heat the oven to 140°C fan oven/160°C electric oven and brush a couple of baking trays with oil. Knead the poppy seed dough until it is pliable, and then divide the mixture into balls slightly smaller than a cherry. Roll them in poppy seeds in a small bowl, and arrange spaced slightly apart on a baking tray. Repeat the process with the sesame seed dough, this time rolling the balls into slightly elongated lozenge shapes and coating them in sesame seeds. Slice the roll of cheese dough into discs about 1cm thick. Bake the biscuits for 35–40 minutes until the cheese ones are lightly golden, by which time the others will also be cooked. Loosen the cheese biscuits with a palette knife, and leave them all to cool. They will keep well for up to a week in an airtight container.

Stocks

It is a rare soup that can hold its head high with no more than water as its foundation, although there are exceptions, chilled soups such as gazpachos and others that contain enough cream or yogurt to distract from a stock's absence. Hence the majority of recipes in this book call for a broth or stock that gives the soup ingredients a platform on which to shine. But there is nothing to daunt the cook, there is a route to suit every occasion depending on the circumstances.

Undoubtedly the best stock will be one that is made by your own fair hands, but this kind of attention to detail rests on a sliding scale in my kitchen, and I only run to chicken on a regular basis. Thankfully though, this is the most useful, so I always make a pot as a matter of course after a roast chicken. And latterly I have also become married to the Deluxe chicken stock (see page 171), where you not only end up with a beautifully succulent poached chicken and lightly cooked pot vegetables, but two sets of stock - the first being the cooking liquor, with a second stock made from the carcass once you've stripped the chicken.

Further down the scale, the main consideration is whether you use a shop-bought fresh stock or dried stock in the form of powder or cubes – but contrary to what we might hope for and expect, the first is not necessarily better than the second.

What flavour?

The principal stocks called for in the recipes are either chicken or vegetable, fish stocks and very occasionally beef. Of these, I only make chicken from scratch on a regular basis, even though I have given recipes for making vegetable and fish stocks should you choose. And if you do happen to find yourself in possession of a lovely pile of beef or veal bones, then simply apply the same method as for chicken. I have never had any success making lamb stock, however, it is difficult to successfully rid it of fat, and the resulting flavour tends to be disappointing. As does duck for the same reason, while pheasant I find too strong, but guinea fowl and turkey are both an excellent alternative to chicken. And a stock made with ham hocks or the cooking liquor from poaching a gammon make an excellent base for lentils and dried pea soups, providing they are not too salty.

Convenience fresh stock

While a 'fresh' stock is likely to be superior to dried if it is homemade, many shop-bought 'fresh' stocks are actually inferior to cubes or powder. Sadly what began as an excellent form of convenience, has been hijacked by some of the larger food producers, whose 'fresh' stocks today are even more replete with flavour enhancers and chemicals than dried ones, they have simply been reconstituted. It is the difference between a carton of freshly squeezed orange juice and one that is made from concentrate, that is packaged and sold in a way that deceives the consumer into thinking they are buying the real thing.

So when shopping for fresh stock, always read the label to check the ingredients, and beware of words like 'hydrolysed', the addition of flavour enhancers and preservatives, bearing in mind that if it is not up to scratch and that is all that is on offer, you will do better with a good brand of dried stock.

Two fresh stocks to look out for are Joubere, and Sainsbury's, who were the first to introduce them. When good, they are a great convenience. I usually keep a few pots in the freezer, shown a hot tap and then gently reheated in a saucepan you have a fine stock in minutes.

Stock cubes and powders

The main caution with dried stocks lies in the amount and type of salt they contain. Aside from the obvious problem of unwittingly adding more salt to a soup than you intended, the type of salt contained in cubes and powders is rarely up to much. Used in any quantity poor salt can cast an artificial, almost chemical, flavour into the soup. But most soups do need some salt to bring out their character, and the cleanest flavour will be provided by a good sea salt such as Maldon. So when possible go for a stock cube or powder that advertises 'low salt' or 'reduced salt', but otherwise it is best to go easy and only use them in small amounts, or alternatively make them up to half the strength suggested.

This said I wouldn't be without a pot of Marigold Swiss vegetable bouillon, that in addition to the standard comes in various forms – organic, vegan, and reduced salt, which is my preferred pot. Knorr stock cubes are also a useful route to beef, lamb, chicken and fish broths, bearing in mind their hefty salt content.

Basic chicken stock

Any household for whom a roast chicken or guinea fowl is a regular feature is well placed here, by making a pot of stock a ritual at the end of the meal, the foundation for the next one is in place. And when that isn't on the menu, many butchers will be happy to give you the chicken trimmings or a carcass for the task, as will mail order suppliers. In this case it is worth roasting the bones first until any skin or flesh is golden, as this provides half the flavour. If, however, you find yourself paying a handsome sum for the trimmings, which I never feel is quite in the spirit, then I would rather roast up and enjoy a tray of chicken wings instead.

Vegetables aren't essential but can be included if you happen to have odds and ends lying around, and it makes sense to pop any half decent trimmings into the pot, but it won't suffer unduly if you don't. What does make a difference is a drop of white wine.

1 chicken carcass, post-roast
a small glass of white wine
sea salt

Place the chicken carcass in a saucepan that will hold it snugly, add the wine and cover with water by 2cm. A great deal of the art lies in bringing it to the boil. It is fine to do this over a high heat, but reduce it to low before it comes to the boil, otherwise you risk a cloudy, for which read greasy, stock. And there is nothing more unappetising than a pot of murky stock in the fridge, it should be a lovely crystal gold.

So having brought it to the edge of a simmer, with just a few small bubbles rising almost imperceptibly, skim off any foam on the surface. Add a good teaspoon of salt and simmer for at least 1 hour, longer if you prefer. Strain the stock and taste it. If it seems at all thin, then pour it back into the pan and cook at a rolling boil to reduce it by up to half its volume. This will concentrate the flavour. Leave it to cool, then cover and chill. If you want to keep it longer than a few days, then simply bring it back to the boil which will kill off any bacteria likely to taint its flavour. A jellied stock is always a good sign that you have a good rich broth. Either way skim off any fat from the surface before using it.

Deluxe chicken stock

I can but look with envy at the Spanish who can buy special packs of ingredients ready for the stock pot – a selection of vegetables, chicken offcuts, a pork knuckle perhaps and cuts of veal or beef. One of the most delicious soups I have eaten of late was at the house of a Mallorcan, Maria Font, who used such a stock as the basis for 'dirty rice', spiced with a local pork blood sausage *butifarron* and another chilli one called *sobrasada*, with rice and shreds of chicken and pork fillet that cooked in with the stock, and all manner of vegetable goodies but in particular she includes artichokes and broad beans.

When a stock is this good, it has any number of potential lives thereafter as the starting point for adding other ingredients, either in the Mallorcan tradition or in a Japanese one with noodles and a few lightly fried or grilled ingredients, some sliced spring onions or chopped herbs, or looking to Italy with some fluffy dumplings or gnocchi and a shower of Parmesan.

In the absence of such stock-pot materials, I struggle with the idea of sacrificing a whole chicken to the pot, not unusual in professional kitchens, but here you get a delicious *poule au pot* thrown in, or, simply a great deal of very fine stock, and delicate shreds of chicken and vegetables that can be rejigged at the table in any number of ways.

For those with time on their side (it takes some four hours in a very low oven, although minutes to assemble), it is a fine investment. The stock itself is superb, golden and lightly gelled once chilled. Cooked at such a low temperature it does not boil or simmer in the usual fashion, which can risk the fat boiling back into the broth and muddying the flavour and appearance. I normally allow a 1.6kg chicken for four people, so here a 2kg bird will do you for six.

1 x 1.6–2kg free-range chicken, untrussed
groundnut oil for coating
sea salt, black pepper
2 good-sized carrots, trimmed, peeled and
    thickly sliced diagonally
1 celery heart, trimmed and thickly
    sliced diagonally

2 leeks, trimmed and thickly sliced diagonally
1 head of garlic, top sliced off
a few sprigs of thyme tied with string
1 bay leaf
200ml white wine
crème fraîche and coarsely chopped flat-leaf
    parsley to serve for a poule au pot

Heat the oven to 110°C fan oven/130°C electric oven. Heat a large frying pan over a medium-high heat, lightly coat the chicken all over with oil using your hands, season and sear to colour it on all sides – this will provide a little extra flavour for the broth.

Place it in a large casserole and surround it with the vegetables and herbs, add the wine and 1.3 litres water, and a little seasoning. Cover and pop into the oven for 4 hours, by which time the bird should be meltingly tender. By making it a day in advance, you can leave it to cool and then chill it, which allows for skimming off any fat on the surface before using it. Otherwise, using the lid, pour off the cooking liquor and skim off any visible fat on the surface.

If, however, you want to make a classic *poule au pot*, then use only 800ml water, and boil to reduce by about a third to concentrate the flavour, then pour this back over the chicken and vegetables. Carve the bird and serve in warm shallow bowls with the vegetables and juices, with a large dollop of crème fraiche on top and lots of parsley scattered over.

Stocks

Vegetable stock

A vegetable stock is the quickest of brews, and here you can add all your treasured finds to the pot with impunity. The vegetables are cooked for a mere 15 minutes, you can purée them with lots of extra virgin olive oil or salty butter, and you have a lovely sauce to serve with grilled lamb chops or roasted chicken legs. Two dishes that can be made in the time of one must be cause for celebration.

This is just a suggested list of veggies, and I would weight it so the stronger ones like fennel and celery are quantities smaller than the others.

about 1kg (prepared weight) of diced carrot,   *a small glass of white wine*
*   leek, celery, onion, fennel, swede, celeriac,*   *a few sprigs of thyme*
*   tomato*   *sea salt, black pepper*
2 garlic cloves, peeled and finely chopped

Place all the ingredients in a large saucepan, and cover with water by about 3cm. Bring to the boil, and simmer over a low heat for 15 minutes. Strain, reserving the stock, leave this to cool, then cover and chill until required.

Vegetable purée
Discard the thyme and purée the remaining vegetables with some extra virgin olive oil or butter and salt. Pass through a sieve, cover and leave to cool if not using straight away, then chill.

Fish stock

This one has a cultural weighting. If you are in France the wherewithal will not be a problem and trimmings are likely to be available at the fishmonger. But otherwise, if you ring through to your fishmonger a couple of days in advance and ask them to save some trimmings for you, hopefully they will be happy to oblige.

1kg fresh fish trimmings (heads and bones),   *1 clove*
*   sole, turbot, plaice, shellfish, etc.*   *a squeeze of lemon juice*
300ml white wine   *a few parsley stalks*
1 onion, peeled and chopped   *sea salt*

Place the fish trimmings in a large saucpan with the wine, add water to just cover and bring slowly to the boil. Skim the stock and add the onion, clove, a squeeze of lemon juice, the parsley stalks and a little salt. Simmer the stock for 30 minutes, then strain. Leave to cool, then cover and chill until required.

Soup-making kit

Liquidisers

This particular kitchen workhorse would seem to have lost its way in recent years. My own theory as to why lies with the success of a sleek glass American bar-style blender, designed for crushing ice and making cocktails, that became a 'must-have' for the design-conscious cook in the 1980s. Following suit, every other kitchen appliance manufacturer started to make their blenders in keeping with this retro model. The problem being, the original was never designed for making soup. With a lid that pushes on and lifts off with equal ease, when used to purée soups this habitually flies off, even when held in place with a tea towel over the top and considerable force. They are, at best, messy, showering hot soup over everything in sight, and at worst they are dangerous, placing the user at risk of scalding.

So if buying a blender, check that the lid does actually screw or lock into place. This may well mean going for function over looks, but it is a small price to pay. One manufacturer who always seems to have at least one design of blender offering this feature is Kenwood. But otherwise, a company's customer services should be able to provide you with this information.
www.kenwood.co.uk

Food processors

While a liquidiser is the means to achieving a silky smooth soup, the food processer comes increasingly into play with the rise in appreciation of textured soups. I especially love soups that offer an array of textures, where you set aside some of the vegetables, and pulse the remainder, before combining the two. I have long been dependent on my Magimix, as close as I am ever likely to get to an assistant. One of the 'Compact' models, it does everything the bigger ones do without taking up too much space.
www.magimix.com

Wand blenders

One of the quickest routes to puréeing a soup is a wand or stick blender, providing you are happy with a little texture, as they never purée to the silky finish of a liquidiser. The original is still the best, the Bamix.
www.bamix-blender.co.uk

Storage

Lock & Lock containers that have wings on the lid that clip onto the base, the original of their type, are indispensable to the soup cook. Great for storing stocks in the fridge, transporting soups and for freezing them, you can rest assured that not so much as a drop of liquid will find its way out.
www.johnlewis.co.uk and www.jwpltd.co.uk

ajo blanco 152
almonds:
    ajo blanco 152
    broccoli and almond soup 23
    mint and almond pesto 40
antipasti 162
apples:
    beetroot and apple soup 40–1
aubergine soup, curried 50
avocados:
    chilled avocado soup 13

bacon:
    bacon and sage dumplings 158–9
    broad bean soup with basil 23
    pot au feu 116
    Puy lentil, spinach and bacon
        soup 134–5
    tomato cup-a-soup 26
barley:
    ham and barley soup 140
    Scotch broth 140
basic chicken stock 170
beans:
    beans on toast soup 160
    bruschetta with butter bean purée 10
    pistou 144
    quick fasolada 136
    ribollita 155
    Turkish village soup 158
beef:
    beetroot bouillon with steak 109
    pot au feu 116
    skinny beef 34
    spinach and beef stew 110
beetroot:
    beetroot and apple soup 40–1
    beetroot and pomegranate soup 51
    beetroot bouillon 109
bigos 104
biscuits:
    cocktail shortbreads 167
    pear and Stilton soup 48
borlotti beans:
    ribollita 155
    Turkish village soup 158
bouillabaisse 90–2
bourride 86–7
bread:
    ajo blanco 152
    bacon and sage dumplings 158–9
    beans on toast soup 160
    bruschetta with butter bean purée 10
    crab toasts 16

croutons 68, 86, 165
garlic bread 165
garlic soup 156
gazpacho 154
goat's cheese toasties 51, 134
oven-baked French onion soup 160
pappa al pomodoro 162
pitta toasts 166
rarebits 166
ribollita 155
toasted Cheddar sarnies 52
Turkish village soup 158
broad beans:
    broad bean and chicken stew 118
    broad bean soup with basil 23
broccoli:
    broccoli and almond soup 23
    grilled broccoli and sesame salad 37
bruschetta with butter bean purée 10
butter bean purée, bruschetta with 10
butternut squash:
    butternut squash soup with nutmeg
        and ginger 27
    butternut squash soup with truffle
        cream 68
    lamb and butternut stew 114–15

cabbage:
    coleslaw 34
    speedy chickpea and cabbage soup 144
    Turkish village soup 158
cannellini beans:
    quick fasolada 136
carrots:
    chunky carrot, saffron and coriander
        soup 32
    cream of carrot soup 74
cauliflower:
    cauliflower and coriander soup 34
    cauliflower cheese soup 56
    pork and cauliflower stew 108
    white vegetable soup 72
cavolo nero, bruschetta with butter bean
    purée and 10
celeriac and grainy mustard soup 30
celery soup with Camembert 55
cheese:
    cauliflower cheese soup 56
    celery soup with Camembert 55
    feta and dill pitta toasts 166
    French green lentil soup
        with Roquefort 136
    goat's cheese toasties 51, 134
    leafy green soup with feta

and olives 56–7
    oven-baked French onion soup 160
    pear and Stilton soup 48
    rarebits 166
    spinach soup with ricotta 29
    sweet potato and cumin soup with
        feta yogurt 58
    toasted Cheddar sarnies 52
    white cheese pastries 46
cherry soup, Russian 46
chicken:
    basic chicken stock 170
    bigos 104
    broad bean and chicken stew 118
    chicken and mushroom noodle pot 119
    chicken brochettes 65
    chicken mulligatawny 112
    chicken noodle soup 124
    chicken stock 170–1
    deluxe chicken stock 171
    five-spice chicken sticks 37
    poule au pot 120
    spicy coconut chicken soup 123
    warming chicken and rice soup 62
chickpea and cabbage soup 144
chillies:
    mussel soup with tomato and chilli 82
    spicy red lentil soup 130
    sweetcorn and chilli soup 30–1
chorizo sausage:
    bigos 104
    pea and chorizo pitta toasts 166
chowder:
    a chowder pie 85
    seabass and mussel chowder 77
    smoked haddock and potato
        chowder 77
cocktail shortbreads 167
coconut milk:
    chicken mulligatawny 112
    curried coconut yogurt soup 64
    spicy coconut chicken soup 123
coleslaw 34
consommé, tomato 10–11
coriander:
    cauliflower and coriander soup 34
    chilled cucumber and coriander soup 60
    chunky carrot, saffron and coriander
        soup 32
courgette soup, summer's day 12
crab:
    crab and fennel soup 74
    crab toasts 16
    Normandy fish soup 88

croutons 68, 86, 165
cucumber:
    chilled cucumber and coriander soup 60
    gazpacho 154
    raita 50
curried aubergine soup 50
curried coconut yogurt soup 64
curried smoked haddock and potato
    stew 83

deluxe chicken stock 171
duck, smoked 152
dumplings, bacon and sage 158–9

eggs:
    egg-fried rice 95
    garlic soup with a poached egg 156
equipment 173

fasolada, quick 136
favourite tomato soup 24
fennel:
    crab and fennel soup 74
feta and dill pitta toasts 166
fish:
    a chowder pie 85
    a simple bouillabaisse 90–2
    bourride 86–7
    crab and fennel soup 74
    crab toasts 16
    cream of fennel soup with grilled
        scallops 74
    curried smoked haddock and potato
        stew 83
    garlic butter mussel pot 78
    moules marinière 83
    mussel soup with tomato and chilli 82
    Normandy fish soup 88
    pea soup with squid 76
    Portuguese fish stew 98
    prawn brochettes 138
    Provençal red mullet soup 80
    romesco de peix 93
    salmon and saffron broth 95
    seabass and mussel chowder 77
    smoked haddock and potato
        chowder 77
    smoked salmon 13
    stock 172
    Thai hot and sour soup 96
    white vegetable soup with smoked
        haddock 72
five-spice chicken sticks 37
flageolet beans:

pistou 144
food processors 173
French green lentil soup 136
frisee:
    lentil, lamb and frisee broth 107

garlic:
    garlic bread 165
    garlic butter mussel pot 78
    garlic *raita* 130
    garlic soup with a poached egg 156
    see also wild garlic
gazpacho 154
goat's cheese toasties 51, 134
grapes:
    ajo blanco 152
green minestrone 40

ham:
    ham and barley soup 140
    ham hock and split pea soup 146
haricot beans:
    beans on toast soup 160
harira 102

jellied red pepper and tequila soup 14

lamb:
    harira 102
    lamb and butternut stew 114–15
    lentil, lamb and frisee broth 107
    Persian rhubarb soup 107
    Scotch broth 140
leafy green soup 56–7
leeks:
    leek and potato soup 19
    potage parmentier 19
    spicy red lentil soup 130
    vichyssoise 16
lentils:
    French green lentil soup 136
    lentil, lamb and frisee broth 107
    Middle Eastern lentil soup 128
    Nada's Syrian grain soup 132
    plum tomato soup with
        green lentils 138
    Puy lentil, spinach and bacon
        soup 134–5
    spicy red lentil soup 130–1
    two lentil soup with caramelised onions
        and lemon 137
    very Monterey soup 128
liquidisers 173

Middle Eastern lentil soup 128
mint and almond pesto 40
moules marinière 83
mushrooms:
    chicken and mushroom noodle pot 119
    double mushroom soup 42
    Russian mushroom soup 143
mussels:
    garlic butter mussel pot 78
    moules marinière 83
    mussel soup with tomato and chilli 82
    romesco de peix 93
    seabass and mussel chowder 77
    Thai hot and sour soup 96

Nada's Syrian grain soup 132
noodles: chicken and mushroom
        noodle pot 119
    chicken noodle soup 124
Normandy fish soup 88

olives:
    antipasti 162
    leafy green soup with 56–7
    spinach and beef stew with 110
onions:
    oven-baked French onion soup 160
    two lentil soup with caramelised onions
        and lemon 137
    white onion soup 38
oregano croutons 165

pak choi:
    Thai hot and sour soup 96
pancetta:
    wintery spelt soup 133
pappa al pomodoro 162
paprika, thyme and olive oil
        pitta toasts 166
parsley soup with saffron cream 66–7
parsnip soup 38
pastries, white cheese 46
pear and Stilton soup 48
peas:
    chunky pea soup 20–1
    pea and chorizo pitta toasts 166
    pea soup with squid 76
    peas 'n rice soup 148
    see also split peas
peppers:
    jellied red pepper and tequila soup 14
    romesco de peix 93
    rouille 92
    two pepper soup 36

Index

Persian rhubarb soup 107
pesto, mint and almond 40
pie, chowder 85
pistou 144
pitta toasts 166
plum tomato soup 138
pomegranate:
    beetroot and pomegranate soup 51
    broad bean and chicken stew with
        pomegranate 118
    Middle Eastern lentil soup with
        pomegranate syrup 128
pork and cauliflower stew 108
Portuguese fish stew 98
pot au feu 116
potage parmentier 19
potatoes:
    curried smoked haddock and potato
        stew 83
    leek and potato soup 19
    Portuguese fish stew 98
    potage parmentier 19
    a simple bouillabaisse 90–2
    smoked haddock and potato
        chowder 77
    sweet potato and cumin soup 58
    vichyssoise 16
    wild garlic soup 20
poule au pot 120
prawns:
    a chowder pie 85
    pea soup with squid 76
    prawn brochettes 138
    Thai hot and sour soup 96
Provençal red mullet soup 80
prunes:
    bigos 104
Puy lentil, spinach and bacon soup 134–5

radish salad 13
raita:
    raita 50
    garlic *raita* 130
rarebits 166
red gurnard:
    Normandy fish soup 88
red mullet soup, Provençal 80
red snapper:
    bourride 86–7
rhubarb soup, Persian 107
ribollita 155
rice:
    egg-fried rice 95
    peas 'n rice soup 148

Persian rhubarb soup 107
    warming chicken and rice soup 62
ricotta, spinach soup with 29
rocket salad 152
romesco de peix 93
rouille 92
Russian cherry soup 46
Russian mushroom soup 143

salads:
    coleslaw 34
    grilled broccoli and sesame salad 37
    radish salad 13
    rocket salad 152
salmon and saffron broth 95
sauerkraut:
    bigos 104
scallops:
    cream of carrot soup with grilled
        scallops 74
    a simple bouillabaisse 90–2
Scotch broth 140
seabass:
    seabass and mussel chowder 77
    a simple bouillabaisse 90–2
seabream:
    romesco de peix 93
    a simple bouillabaisse 90–2
shortbreads, cocktail 167
smoked haddock:
    a chowder pie 85
    curried smoked haddock and potato
        stew 83
    smoked haddock and potato
        chowder 77
    white vegetable soup with 72
smoked salmon 13
spelt soup, wintery 133
spinach:
    chilled spinach and yogurt soup 60
    Puy lentil, spinach and bacon
        soup 134–5
    salmon and saffron broth 95
    spinach and beef stew 110
    spinach soup with ricotta 29
split peas:
    ham hock and split pea soup 146
    harira 102
spring vegetable soup 66
squid:
    Normandy fish soup 88
    pea soup with squid 76
stews:
    broad bean and chicken stew 118

curried smoked haddock and potato
    stew 83
lamb and butternut stew 114–15
pork and cauliflower stew 108
Portuguese fish stew 98
spinach and beef stew 110
stocks 169–72
storage 173
summer's day courgette soup 12
sweet potato and cumin soup 58
sweetcorn and chilli soup 30–1
Syrian meze 132

Thai hot and sour soup 96
tomatoes:
    beans on toast soup 160
    favourite tomato soup 24
    gazpacho 154
    mussel soup with tomato and chilli 82
    pappa al pomodoro 162
    plum tomato soup 138
    Provençal red mullet soup 80
    Puy lentil, spinach and bacon
        soup 134–5
    quick fasolada 136
    ribollita 155
    spicy red lentil soup 130–1
    tinned tomato soup 24
    tomato consommé 10–11
    tomato cup-a-soup 26
    Turkish village soup 158
truffle cream, butternut squash soup
    with 68
Turkish village soup 158

vegetable stock 172
very Monterey soup 128
vichyssoise 16

wand blenders 173
watercress soup 52–3
white cheese pastries 46
white onion soup 38
white vegetable soup 72
wild garlic soup 20
wintery spelt soup 133

yogurt:
    chilled cucumber and coriander soup 60
    chilled spinach and yogurt soup 60
    curried coconut yogurt soup 64
    spring vegetable soup with yogurt 66
    sweet potato and cumin soup with feta
        yogurt 58